HOW TO MAKE
HORROR
MOVIE TRAILERS

TOM GETTY

ACROLIGHT PICTURES LLC

Acrolight Pictures
An imprint of Acrolight Pictures *LLC*

THIS IS AN ACROLIGHT PICTURES LLC BOOK
PUBLISHED BY TOM GETTY

Copyright © 2022 Acrolight Pictures LLC

This edition published 2022 by Acrolight Pictures LLC.

Press, Johnstown, Pennsylvania

LCCN: 2022909380
ISBN: 978-0-9974800-6-1

Designed by Tom Getty

FIRST EDITION

To my sister, Colleen Hepler

Contents

INTRODUCTION

The Motion Picture Association of America states that over 700 films were released in 2019. Of those films, according to The Numbers, a box office data website, 7.19% were horror films. That's 40 out of the 700 films. Across those 40 choices, horror fans purchased over 88 million tickets. The top scary films of that year included IT: CHAPTER II, ANNABELLE COMES HOME, SCARY STORIES TO TELL IN THE DARK, and MIDSOMMAR, among others. The films contributed to a robust market.

Then Coronavirus struck, the World Health Organization declared a pandemic, and theaters ground to a halt. Horror ticket sales dipped to a little over 63 million. By 2021, surprisingly, the number of horror films released each year…grew to 12.68%. There were more horror movies, but less people seeing those movies. Other genres more than likely fared a similar fate. More movies, less tickets sold. Growing competition for less dollars.

Of course, the video on demand market grew in response. While theaters re-opened, people continued watching movies at home, in even more numbers than before. According to the Motion Picture Association of America, the number of online video streaming services subscriptions around the world tallied 1.1 billion in 2020.

Experts expect the market to grow 8.28% by 2026, according to Statista. People will continue to watch movies; fans will continue to consume horror films. But with a shifting viewing arena, with a dysmorphia of the theatrical market, comes an equalizing of competition. Put another way, horror filmmakers are no longer competing each year against 40 other horror movies. They're likely competing against *hundreds of other entries*, as the data listed earlier only accounts for theatrical releases.

Or, put still another way, horror filmmakers who once utilized the home video market to sell their wares must suddenly deal with the influx of high budget refugees. Studio films now bypassing the theatrical market, making inroads against what was once a fertile trade for aspiring movie directors looking to leverage the genre. For those likely reading this book, filmmakers armed with a horror motion picture ready for distribution, the competition has become even more complex. More invasive, incisive, ruthless. Studios bypassing the theatrical market, turning their eyes to the home video terrain, assaulting the digital landscape with their usual media blitzkrieg of marketing and promotion. Not only does the independent horror filmmaker now compete against the high budgets of studio films, he or she also engages against the exhorbiant marketing budgets of those same studio films. At least in the "old days," filmmakers only competed with the home video marketing budgets. Now, they must war against the theatrical-level marketing budgets—used on home video.

The effect devastates. A studio releases its trailer, it gears audiences up to look for the film on Netflix, or Hulu, or Amazon Prime, Vudu, iTunes, or any of the chosen video-on-demand services; eyeballs shift to those platforms, fans click, the algorithims wrench into high gear—competition is crushed. What once had a chance on home video, now must make room for those 40 studio offerings. Now horror filmmakers directly compete against the titans, rather than the after-market of those titans. The competition will force a reckoning for filmmakers.

Either compete with the studio offerings—or perish.

Worse still, there are always new filmmakers looking to gain entry into the world of filmmaking, anchoring the horror genre to make up for a lack of stars or big budget. Each year, in addition to the studio offerings, there are countless, hundreds—perhaps thousands—of indie horror films, flooding the market services of Netflix, Amazon, Hulu, iTunes, all jumping at the charts, all falling like flies, all plummeting into the abyss of aloritithms programmed for high-engagement.

Films must stand out—or die.

The algorithms that beat the heart-rate of streaming services will ensure it.

Films—horror films especially, which often come saddled with a dearth of stars and budget—must now participate in a radically altered media landscape, one dominated by short attention spans, ever-increasing audience cynicism, ruthless mathematics, and more movies. A film, today, must overcome mountain-ranges of odds to engage, prevail, and endure.

How will the major studios respond to this? As they always have: spend more money.

Not on movies, of course.

But on their marketing.

Tomorrow's winner of today's movie-war will be the one who recognizes this one single fact: ***movies are a marketing business, not a moviemaking one.***

The problem is not better movies, or bigger ones—it's more effectively marketed movies.

Not well-made movies. But rather, well-marketed movies.

Once upon a time, a quality horror film like THE EXORCIST could make its way through word of mouth. It would have the time. There was simply no other films like it.

Now, it would die on a vine.

There are too many exorcisms, too many head-turning demons, too many shouting priests, to create any kind of word of mouth from content alone.

The day of the quality horror blockbuster is over.

The day of the well-marketed horror blockbuster is here to stay.

Notable horror movies today will not be because of their quality—*but because they survived the programming of Silicon Valley.*

How is an indie filmmaker—or any filmmaker, studio-backed or not, supposed to compete?

If a film can't succeed on its quality—then what is it to succeed on?

Simply, its trailer.

A movie, today, succeeds on its trailer.

Nothing more.

If it's not in the trailer, the movie is a goner.

The studios, of course, know this already. Which is why they enlist the chief marketing agencies of the world to craft their films' trailers. The most financially successful studios ensure that each one of their films come armed with at least one blockbuster-level trailer. Sometimes two, or more. Sometimes an entire campagain of trailers, with teasers, TV spots, and social media teases.

They do this beecause they know the truth.

Today, it's all about the trailer.

Movies, today, are about their trailers.

The studios, fiduciary as they are to Wall Street, ensure that everything goes into their trailers—and that nothing is left out.

It's in the trailer. Not the movie.

This goes just as much for horror films as it does for any other type of movie.

It's the quality of the trailer, not the quality of the movie.

But what is a trailer? A simple question—but if the quality of most indepdent films' trailers is any indicator, then it bears asking. Is it a "greatest hits" of a film? A clip reel? What goes into a trailer that makes it so? Furthermore, what goes into it that makes it a *blockbuster* movie trailer—and not just a run-of-the-mill one that doesn't even hit the radar?

The word 'trailer' is unfortunate. Ask any normal person—normal in that they aren't in the industry, that they lead a life outside the purview of movies, that they belong more to the 'audience' category than the 'filmmaker' one—and they'll say that a trailer is a carriage that trails a utility truck. That it's not a commercial for future entertainment. Not a two-minute sampling of a larger film.

But, trailers are what they are.

Trailers.

Named that way because they, used to, trail the film reels of the main showing.

We're stuck with the word.

Trailers.

Simply, they are movie-advertisements.

But what does it mean to *advertise?*

The question plagues the filmmaker trying to produce a trailer for his film. Or at least, it will come to plague him. Because the filmmaker trying to make a trailer for his own film, trying to compete with the blockbuster trailers, will eventually come up short.

Simply the difference between a run-of-the-mill trailer and a blockbuster one is that one is a mini-movie, the other is a sales piece.

The blockbuster trailer producers know they are not producing trailers—they are making sales letters. As such, they utilize a completely different skillset when crafting their trailers. They deploy sales technique, not artistic merit. They understand the age-old principles of attention, interest, desire, and action. The blockbuster trailer makers, with their trailers, direct attention, garner interest, conjure desire, and motivate action. Sales. Not artistic expression.

With horror, it's just the same.

A horror trailer promotes, it does not entertain.

A blockbuster horror trailer directs attention, it does not get it. The trailer is not an end in of itself; it is a means to transfer people over to not just watching the movie but paying to watch the movie. The blockbuster horror trailer maker knows that people pay to see a movie—not to have seen it.

The trailer producer, following the blockbuster tenets, creates expectation—not curiosity. He knows that to arouse curiosity is not enough. He knows that the difference between the two is profound, gulf-like—one bemuses, the other excites and directs. The trailer producer does his work by triangulating desire around the arousal of concrete expectations; expectations that demand fulfillment; fulfillment only possible by paying to watch the movie. As stated in *How To Make Blockbuster Movie Trailers*, a good trailer places expectations in the mind of the viewer; expectation is what stirs the imagination.

Moviegoing is an act of the imagination, just as much as it is a physical one.

The trailer producer knows that a trailer sells story—not mystery. He doesn't concern himself with spoilers, or "giving too much away." He knows the audience wants information, and that they need that information to build a mental model in their minds, their imagination, for what they're paying to see. Spoilers and all.

People want to know what they're getting into. The whole reason for watching the trailer.

This holds doubly true for horror.

Which is why a specific book has been written for the horror genre.

The horror trailer producer must hold specific skills in making not only good trailers, but trailers that compete against the competition as highlighted earlier.

The following pages aim to construct the steps in not only creating great movie trailers, but great horror movie trailers. The book examines all the great horror movie trailers, and provides ample evidence from them, illuminating the concepts of how to create a blockbuster horror trailer from scrap. One that competes. One that wins.

Chapter 1, "The Scary Appeal," looks at the universal appeal that makes all scary films palatable and attractive to audiences. Throughout time. Simply, what motivates people to be scared? Chapter 2, "Selling Horror," looks at arranging the most fundamental aspect of a trailer: its dialogue. Chapter 3, "The Horror Genre," examines the tenets of the horror genre, and why it's important to know them when making a trailer. Chapter 4, "The Problem of Rhythm" highlights the underlying motions of a scary trailer—how fast or slow it should go, and what makes it move. Chapter 5, "Scary Sounds," looks at the most important part of any scary movie trailer: its sound. And how to create it. Chapter 6, "Editing," studies how to find "trailer worthy" shots and edit them together into a top-flight trailer. Chapter 7, "Spooky Words," looks at the concept of copywriting, and how it applies to writing taglines, why it's an essential art to learn and master. Chapter 8, "Designing Titles," looks at how to turn that copy into an aesthetically scary design befitting of a blockbuster horror trailer. Chapter 9, "Mixing" covers the art of mixing and mastering. Chapter 10, "The Last Man on Earth" provides a step-by-step case study in the making of a trailer for an old Vincent Price horror film.

This book aims to provide a structure upon which future horror filmmakers, executives, anyone interested in creating—and selling—horror films—can craft excellent, high-selling horror movie trailers. This book is about making blockbuster horror trailers. Trailers that sell the fear, that bring in the audiences, and create horror classics.

1

THE SCARY APPEAL

The most difficult aspect of creating a movie trailer is coming up with an appeal. Simply, what is being "sold" when selling horror? Subject matter that no one in their right mind would talk about in everyday, normal conversation. Bring horror up to anyone, and they will generally react with disgust and dismissal. They don't watch "those kinds of films."

But the numbers say otherwise.

ALIEN, for instance, a film famous for its chest-busting scene, clocked in over a quarter of a billion dollars, adjusted for inflation. GREMLINS, despite its cuddly focal point, shows hordes of nasty little creatures all acting in horrible, ugly ways. The film made almost half a billion, adjusted for inflation. IT (2017), which depicts a ravenous, evil clown who terrorizes his victims in all sorts of heinous ways—dismemberment, for one—grossed almost half a billion dollars. THE EXORCIST, which spells out the demonic torment of a 12-year-old girl, among other lurid subject matter, made a billion, adjusted for inflation. JAWS, with its blood-thirsty sea creature dismembering adults and children alike, made over a billion, again adjusted for inflation. The SAW films, combined, with its depictions of merciless torture, as well made over a billion. The RESIDENT EVIL films grossed $1.2 billion. THE CONJUR-ING films, with 8 entries, conquered at the worldwide box office over $2 billion.

Highest Grossing Horror, Adjusted For Inflation (Domestic) (Forbes)

1. Jaws (1975) **($1.154 billion)**
2. The Exorcist (1973) **($996.5 million)**
3. Ghostbusters (1984) **($641.3 million)**
4. The Sixth Sense (1999) **($518.8 million)**
5. Gremlins (1984) **($409.8 million)**
6. It (2017) **($328.9 million)**
7. Jaws 2 (1978) **($312.8 million)**
8. The Amityville Horror (1979) **($310.3 million)**
9. Alien (1979) **($286.4 million)**
10. Scary Movie (2000) **($262.5 million)**
11. What Lies Beneath (2000) **($259.9 million)**
12. The Omen (1976) **($257.7 million)**
13. Ghostbusters II (1989) **($255.3 million)**
14. The Blair Witch Project (1999) **($249.3 million)**
15. Poltergeist (1982) **($234.8 million)**
16. Interview with the Vampire (1994) **($226.4 million)**
17. Aliens (1986) **($206.8 million)**
18. Scream (1996) **($203.2 million)**
19. The Ring (2002) **($200.1 million)**
20. Scream 2 (1997) **($197.3 million)**

Indeed, people do watch those kinds of films. Then, and now. But why?

The answer: general audiences are universally attracted to stories about a person or group of people in external conflict with an evil force, told through consistent time, and a consistent reality. In short, audiences are drawn to stories about active good versus active evil, told in a consistent way. Basic, of course. But it is what ties all those high-grossing horror films together. It is the truism, the reliable "formula," if it is one at all, the foundational principle, that glues all the previously mentioned films together. Good versus evil, in consistent time, in consistent reality. The last two are especially important. But what do they both mean?

Consistent Time

The film, while allowing for flashbacks, must be told in a linear fashion; or, at least, the trailer producer must infer with his appeal that time happens in a linear fashion. Time is treated as sacrosanct, an unspoken principle that can't be interfered with. The movie can include flashbacks, as in the character is remembering something, or the film is showing something that previously happened; but the movie cannot butcher the concept of time a la SOUTHLAND TALES, or LOST HIGHWAY, movies where there is very little concept of when or how events are occurring. Examine all the top grossing horror films and you will see that time unfolds in a linear fashion, even if allowing for flashbacks. The audience can, at every step of the way, grasp how time unfolds. This is not to say that the audience must know "what time it is" in a film, it's to say that events, themselves, unfold in a linear, coherent fashion. A movie like MOTHER! would not make the list. A quality film, but its continual violation of time's precepts makes it jarring for most audiences.

Consistent Reality

The film must unfold in a consistent reality; or at least the trailer producer must infer this with his appeal. Once a film establishes a ruling of its existence, it must continue to follow that. It must remain bound by the tenets it establishes of its own story-world. For instance, while seeming to break this rule, the A NIGHT-MARE ON ELM STREET films follow a consistent reality. Freddy Krueger, the series' nightmare-invading villain, while existing in the dream world, can cross over and affect his victims through their nightmares. This is a rule that remains unbroken, unless otherwise specified. In contrast, the quasi-horror film DONNIE DARKO does not follow this rule, to its own quality and effect. Donnie's reality is a shapeshifting, amorphous, oblique blob. The audience, and Donnie, aren't sure what's real and what's fantasy, or dream, or flashback, or another dimension all together. That is the point of the entire film; but its violation of reality disqualifies it for general audiences. Not because of any lack of quality, but because general audiences tend to believe that their own realities unfold in a consistent, causality, effect-based way. This is just a rule of general audiences. Not through any arbitrary means, but as a matter of the human mind, and how it perceives life.

It is a matter of classical storytelling. It is a matter of classical design.

Classical Design

Robert McKee defines the concept as a story about an active character or active group of characters who fight against outside forces of evil, through continuous time, "within a consistent and causally connected fictional reality," to an ending of resolved consequence (McKee, 1997, p. 45).

Classical storytelling is how most people perceive life. They dream in a linear fashion; they remember in a linear fashion. When they tell stories of their own lives, they do so with cause and effect, not willy-nilly hopscotching through time and space. When they consume stories of other people's lives, it's with the preference of that mirroring their own guidelines—whether they aware of those guidelines or not.

Classical storytelling is what defines box office success. If it's hitting "the charts," the upper reaches of the box office, it's due to the story intentionally, or unintentionally, following the tenets of classical storytelling. The horror trailer producer notes this and applies it to his appeals.

The successes of the horror genre follow the principles of classical storytelling. Laurie Strode must evade Michael Myers in HALLOWEEN (1978). She may flashback to her childhood (HALLOWEEN II (1981)), she may find herself paralyzed by fear (internal conflict) but her main strife is with a force decidedly outside of herself: Michael Myers. The same goes for Nancy Thompson of A NIGHTMARE ON ELM STREET (1984); her tormentor may invade her dreams, but it's through very consistent rules that she, along with the audience, must puzzle through. She can figure out Freddy's invasion of her dreamworld, and thus ultimately invert his game: she brings him through to our world. Her story takes place in a consistent time, in a consistent reality. Her efforts are largely active. The same goes for Sidney Prescott of SCREAM, who, while seemingly passive at the outset, takes ever increasing drastic steps to evade, and ultimately vanquish the menacing Ghost Face.

In other examples, The Warrens wage war against unholy spirits in THE CONJURING films, the teenagers of the FRIDAY THE 13TH films must navigate a very definite maze of Camp Crystal Lake as Jason pops up at every turn, the victims of Jigsaw in the

SAW films must struggle their way out of his deadly traps, the normal every-day people of PARANORMAL ACTIVITY must understand the invisible force menacing their lives, the children of IT (2017) must unite to defeat the evil clown; The priest in THE EXORCIST, in spite of his intense inner spiritual qualms, must put everything aside and mount a campaign against the evil that has infected the young Regan character—he must ultimately perish himself to save the girl.

All these films, all the characters of these films, are engaged in active, external conflict with external forces of evil; all of the forces consistent, all of their realities sealed. The evil in these films are bound by rules of a consistent time and reality.

The films may teeter on the verge of reality splintering apart, but they must always come back to externality, causation, consistency. In SHUTTER ISLAND, the Leonardo DiCaprio character sieges an island housing a mental hospital, investigating to find a missing patient. His inquiries lead to him hallucinating, losing track of time, wallowing, questioning his own sanity, having the audience question their own sanity; but ultimately the truth is revealed: the DiCaprio character is the missing patient. The film veers about through time and space, through sanity and insanity, but the external investigation for the missing patient leads the DiCaprio character to consequence of irreversible change—his own lobotomy.

Minimalism

Classical storytelling is, of course, not the only kind of story. It sits at the top of a triangle, a triumvirate, as McKee defines it (1997, p. 57). Below, at the bottom of the triangle lies both minimalism and antiplot. Minimalism, is, as the name suggests, a minimalizing of classical design. Characters are no longer active participants; rather, their conflicts are more internalized, and therefore more seemingly passive. THE EXORCIST highlights a bit of this minimalized conflict with the priest who wrestles with his belief in god (but make no mistake, this battle is overshadowed, and resolved, by the presence of the devil). Evil, the force of antagonism, may loom, but it pales in comparison to the forces within. Characters may struggle against outside forces, but it's their internal battles that count the most. Evil in classical story telling must be the dominating force. In Minimalism, also, there may be multiple characters, with auxiliary desires, divergent pathways—a la, TRICK OR TREAT. Time is not as consistent. Characters drift in and out of recollection. Reality may be consistent, but it may slip into hallucination, dream. The point is to soften against the tenets of classical storytelling, to create a deeper effect. One that general audiences do not always agree with. John Carpenter's THE THING flirts with this with its famously unresolved ending.

Antiplot

Antiplot, on the deeper end of the triangle, represents stories that are reactionary, contradictory to classical storytelling. Here sits a film like TWIN PEAKS: FIRE WALK WITH ME, with its character descending into drugs and insanity, the causality of events uncertain, the character's existence even more so. Director David Lynch is a master of the antiplot, a la MULHOLLAND DRIVE, a film that teeters on madness, and then descends in with a stark plunge. The meaning of such a film is of life's absurdity, its meaninglessness, its tentative grasp in the face of crippling psychological, cosmic, and universal forces—all unknown, unseen, and incomprehensible. This is not a message endorsed by general audiences, despite their obvious thirst for stories of evil forces. Another example of antiplot is DONNIE DARKO. His characterization, while apparent, disintegrates into a series of psychotic episodes, splintering identities, leading him into an unknowable conclusion, and an uncertain future. While horrific, it is not the kind of horror audiences are interested in. Not as any general rule, but as a matter of practice. Audiences tend to believe that their greatest enemy is outside of themselves. Their greatest fear is symbolized, canonized, by a Freddy Kruger, a Michael Myers, a Jigsaw, a mummy, a vampire, a ghost. General audiences believe that their greatest foe is ultimately crystalized outside of themselves as a distinguishable 'other.' They do not, however, suspect the greatest of all enemies: the one inside themselves. Most people will not endorse the idea that the worst enemy they'll ever face resides somewhere in the dark recesses of their own minds, their own souls.

It just does not comport.

The antiplot, while horrific, is a horror of the unraveling that begins inside, the suicidal, endemic to the mind and soul. Psychological horror frequently courts with this, but to be sure, it always circles back to psychiatric explanations, a la SHUTTER ISLAND. The story can take a dip into psychological waters, but it must be ultimately explained away by something.

The unknowable, a film without clear demarcations and resolutions, is a terror too terrifying for general audiences.

The clown in IT may be a stand-in for the children's own internal fear, but make no mistake, once the clown is dispatched, those internal fears, having endured for four decades, are resolved. It, while a formidable foe, is certainly no stand-in for the true terrors of a splintering self and the insanities that can be borne in the mind. Its evil is not ultimate.

That's what's most comforting, if that word can be used, about horror films of the classical variety. The horror is localized outside the characters. It is understandable, knowable, quantifiable. Like the shark in JAWS, it eventually reveals itself in daylight. Like Freddy pulled through the dream-reality barrier in A NIGHT-MARE ON ELM STREET, evil can be cajoled, controlled, and ultimately dispelled. Like the unmasking of Ghost Face at the end of every SCREAM film, evil is simply a force that is 'other,' and ultimately, knowable, ultimately defeatable. Horror films, of the classical variety, are re-assurances of what we believe to be true: we are the ultimate purveyor's of our lives, in pursuit of concrete goals, interfered with only by evil forces who can be summed up in the form a man wearing a ski mask.

Horror, while frightening, can be conquered. The trailer producer includes this with his appeal.

Horror Values

That is not to say that good must always win. In many ways, the popular horror films suggest an endurance of evil. Certainly, the HALLOWEEN films speak to that, with Michael Myers always disappearing into the wind at the end. Certainly, the high number of A NIGHTMARE ON ELM STREET sequels highlight a worldview of evil's persistence. Same goes for the SAW and SCREAM franchise. THE RING certainly doesn't bode for happy times ahead. Nor does THE BIRDS, HALLOWEEN, RESIDENT EVIL, THE OMEN, the AMITYVILLE HORROR films. If those films say anything, it's that evil cannot even be held at bay—it is omnipresent and unnegotiable. Mindless.

Rather, it is to say that horror must follow the strict tenets of classical storytelling—active characters in active conflict with external forces through consistent reality and time, told to a resolute finish. The horror, while sometimes winning, while always enduring, must be an oppression that is outside, knowable, and concrete. Horror, in its ultimate expression, is an accountable force that can be summed up in an icon. The mask, as the popular cliche holds.

It must be outside trying to get in.

It is classical story that unifies the commerce of popular horror film.

It is what the trailer producer must centralize his efforts around. Not the selling of stars, or special effects, or monsters (he shouldn't worry about showing too much of the monster). It is the selling of classical story. His trailer efforts should always highlight, whether true or not, the classical elements of the film in question, of its characters in active conflict, of its consistent reality and time, of its definable force of evil.

It is selling classical horror that this book is most concerned with.

2

SELLING HORROR

It's hard enough to *tell* a horror story in a hundred-plus minutes. It's another to *sell* it in less than two. That is to say, a story must be told—and sold. Look at any advertisement for a horror film—it not only tells a story, but it also sells a story. It presents character, value, scene, act, and antagonism, all in a matter of minutes, and does so in an appealing manner. "Appealing" meaning one that's captivating; "captivating" meaning one that raises the audience's interest and creates a demand in them to know more; demand meaning a movement—or determined movement—to buy tickets, video-on-demands, DVDs, Blu-rays, etc. A "want" to see the picture. A "desire" to find out "what happens." But the compression to less-than-two-minutes invites all kinds of problems. Intrigue, for one. Mystery, for another. How much of the two to put in? Indeed, what to put in at all? And how to order it? Confusion awaits at every turn. Compression is one matter; coherency another; interest, the holy grail. That is, interest enough to create expectation, to stimulate imagination, to cultivate desire to see the film.

Is it enough to tell the trailer producer that he should just, "Create a three-act structure?" Imagine the terror. How does one, looking at the blank canvas, just create a three-act structure, or a one-act structure, or a two-act structure? How does one create any structure at all? And not only structure but present it through the "lens" of horror. Indeed, not only does the trailer producer have to tell and sell—he must present the genre of horror itself. Because unlike a regular trailer, the trailer producer must really highlight that he in fact has a film of horror. But what does it mean to signal to the audience the genre of the film? Are the words "horror" necessary? Or are there codes, signals, implicit in the material itself that signal the designated genre? How can the trailer producer be sure those are coming through?

Telling Story

First, he must claim control over the ability to tell story in a trailer. That begins with first turning off the film's images, doing away with them as quickly as possible. Not permanently, as they will come in handy later. But for now, in creating a structure, in telling a story. At this stage, they serve no purpose other than to confuse, intimidate, and lead astray. The trailer producer, looking to images to tell a story, finds too many interesting pictures, all interpretable, all leading this way and that way, none forming any concrete ideas or expectations. A shot of Dracula, his eyes lit, everything else in shadow, raising his arm at the camera, draws interest—but where to place it? After the shot of the woman? Before? Too many juxtapositions (a word we'll get to) can be formed. Too many stories. Too many rhetorical ideas can be conferred just by shot placement alone.

Best to turn off the images all together. In doing so, the producer looks to isolate the most important artifact of the project: the dialogue. Because it's in the dialogue where, at least now a days, a film's story is directly told. It is the sound, the dialogue, that motivates a motion picture. Not the pictures. If the trailer editor started with the images, cutting in the picture, the best "trailer worthy" shots, he would then have to go back and find dialogue, or some kind of voiceover to support the claims made by the images. That is an almost impossible task. Because the truth is, most films are not first constructed out of their images—they are first written, through a script, through dialogue. For most writers, it is through their characters' words that they are telling a story. And it is story that the trailer producer must be most concerned with.

This is what it means to show and not tell, as the famous dictum goes. Or at least, this is how we begin showing, and not telling. With dialogue, not images. It's within the film's dialogue the trailer producer will discover the ammunition needed to tell the story of the film, and present it, sell it.

Dialogue

To begin, the trailer producer must go through the entire film and find the relevant dialogue. What's relevant? Certainly not everything. There are just too many greetings and salutations. All relevant dialogue will be found in two types. *Exposition* and *action*. Exposition is where someone is giving information about the world of the story. Action is where someone is trying to get something with their words.

Exposition

Consider exposition. This is information that is needed to follow the world of the story. Robert McKee defines it as: "facts—the information about setting, biography, and characterization that the audience needs to know to follow and comprehend the events of the story" (McKee, 1997, p. 334). This is anytime anyone talks about the monster, its creation, the killer, describes the killer, the villain, the antagonism; this is anytime any of the characters describes the horror at stake. Examples of exposition would include:

In the LAND OF THE DEAD trailer when the one character says of the undead, "They're communicating, they're thinking."

In the trailer for SHUTTER ISLAND when the DiCaprio character says, "We are duly appointed federal marshals." Another from that film is when the guard says, "We take only the most dangerous, damaged patients."

In the trailer for HALLOWEEN when Dr. Loomis says, "I spent eight years trying to reach him."

Exposition is information that is necessary to follow the story. Here, in a trailer, it provides the basis for stating a case, for crafting, for shading, for creating. When Dr. Loomis announces that he spent eight years trying to reach "him," the audience picks up that he's talking about someone who is so divorced from reality that he was impervious to a decade of psychoanalysis. When the guard in SHUTTER ISLAND says they take only the most dangerous, damaged patients, the audience implicitly knows, or at least senses, the "duly appointed federal marshals" are entering a world dominated by evil—that the two heroes are already neck deep in horror.

Exposition typically speaks to one of the tenets of storytelling— the setting, character, value, or antagonism. There's a reason every trailer, or so it seems, used to begin with the phrase, "In a world where," or "In a time of." Both phrases spoke to exposition, to setting—a place and a time. In the SCREAM trailer, a voice says, "It all began with a scream over 911" (dialogue used from the end of the movie, incidentally). In the trailer for HEREDITARY, the character says, "...so many strange faces here today." The film takes place in the present. The other Ari Aster film takes place in the present, as the character says in the trailer for MIDSOMMAR, "You've been wanting out of this stupid relationship for, like, a year now." All are ways of highlighting when the film takes place. The exposition in the trailer for MALIGNANT speaks to character, with the central woman saying, "I'm having visions." The DAWN OF THE DEAD (1978) trailer speaks to value, "A horrible, hauntingly accurate vision of the mindless excesses of a society gone mad." In horror movie trailers, the convention is to usually characterize the antagonism; the cliche is always a description of the male monster. "He never utters a word," says the narrator of the FRIDAY THE 13TH PART 4 trailer. "He is not patient," says the narrator of the A NIGHTMARE ON ELM STREET 2 trailer. Even when the narrator was completely dropped from the majority of trailers, the ELM STREET remake continued with the same rhetorical effect, "He is burnt." They are all words to describe antagonism. They are all exposition.

Action

Action-dialogue is when someone is trying to get something with their words. This is wide-ranging. Anything from a character trying to cajole, to an evil force trying to kill, can be used, can provide dramatic impetus, can supply the necessary traction for a trailer. The little girl in THE EXORCIST trailer pleads for her mother. "Somebody help me!" a young woman yells in the remake of THE TEXAS CHAINSAW MASSACRE (2003) trailer. "Sally, I hear something, stop," asks the young man of his sister pushing his wheelchair in the original. "Watch his tail," the fisherman in JAWS commands. "Run!" yells the one woman in THE DESCENT trailer. All of these examples are of characters trying to get something.

Subtext comes into play. Which is the information, the content beneath the words being spoken. The trailer editor must be able to know how to read into what the words are really saying. A phrase like, "Run" is deeply loaded: "Everyone, listen up, we need to move as fast as our bodies will take us because there is something deadly right on our tails, and its designs are on our destruction—run!" "Somebody help me" is also loaded: "To anyone out there listening, I need assistance right now because I am in great danger from chainsaw wielding maniacs!" So, of course, exposition and action can blend. Characters state something about the world, while implicitly asking for something. Characters demand something and as well betray a fact about the world's story. In THE DESCENT trailer, the woman who says, "The batteries on our lights will run out," is stating a fact as well as hurrying the other characters along, time a factor in their survival. The point is to be able to spot one type of dialogue or the other and classify it. The point is to be able to extract these two types of dialogue from the film's runtime and leave behind the rest. Because then the trailer producer will turn toward arranging these two types of dialogue, and their respective collections.

The Arrangement of Dialogue

Armed with the dialogue, the trailer producer can set out formulating a story. Typically, the arrangement of dialogue would be a matter of playing the types of dialogue against one another; a little bit of exposition here, a little bit of action over there. In a well-made trailer, the two balance together, creating a dialectic, an argument almost, a dynamic back and forth that creates drama. "This thing, it's going to follow you," says a guy in the IT FOLLOWS trailer. "Is someone there?" A man asks to the dark in the trailer for SAW.

The first is exposition, the second is action, the character wanting to know if someone is about to pounce on him. Then, "It was the woods themselves; they're alive!" says a young woman in the original EVIL DEAD (1981). The trailer swings back to action-dialogue: "You're all going to die tonight," a possessed girl announces in the trailer for the remake.

First, the trailer producer—the editor really—starts with exposition. He picks out a clip that will set the story, often the vaguest piece of exposition. As a rule, the types of dialogue generally move from the approximate, the vague, to the specific, the germane. The trailer editor needs to, as McKee says, "pace out the exposition." Putting the least important facts at the beginning of the trailer, the most important at the end. First: "100,000 years ago, it found its way into our galaxy," announces the trailer for THE THING (1982). This is a wide span of time, and far away from the film's actual setting; it also scopes the story out to our entire universe. Also, what is "it?" The word "it" is as vague as one can get, and vagueness raises questions. Then, the trailer moves in with, "Trapped in the frozen wasteland of Antarctica." Inch by inch, the exposition dials down, clarifying the concept, the rhetorical device, whatever the trailer is trying to describe. Here, the film's location. Also, the film's monster. What's trapped? Why is it trapped there? The questions raise interest, interest raises desire to know; the effect pulls the audience forward, creating demand, attention.

Second, the trailer editor reaches for action. Again, the same rule applies. Generic to specific. In the case of action, its content is to be found in the subtext. A trailer editor wouldn't typically reach for a phrase like, "Run," saving that for later in the trailer. Instead, the editor, at the beginning of the trailer, looks for actions that are small, indistinct, opaque in subtext. "What did they find?" a woman asks in the trailer for THE THING (2011) remake. She, as well as the audience, wants to know, indeed, what did they find?

The trailer's answer is to supply some exposition: "There's a structure."

Back and forth the pendulum swings. A little bit of exposition. A little bit of action.

The trailer editor moves in, now more specific. "Somebody sent those things here to get us," a character says in the trailer for THE CABIN IN THE WOODS. What things? Why? "You're missing the point," the other character says, "They want to see us punished." Motivation is supplied. "They" is still referred to as "the other," an entity that has yet to be unveiled. "There is something in the fog," a character yells in the trailer for the remake of THE FOG (2005). What could it be?

In the case of horror films, the trailer editor is generally building a characterization of evil; his designs, his arrangement of dialogue, is based around the outlining of an all-powerful force; then, a filling in, a shading, a sharpening of that evil. Generic to specific. A horror trailer is about the building of the monstrous, the nefarious, the sinister, leaving just enough unshaded, leaving the audience wanting more.

Of course, this isn't to broach the subject about "giving it all away" in a trailer. Part of the trailer editor's job is to give it all away, short of the finishing touches. It's not enough to just present odd mystery, vague details, and then leave it at that. The particulars must add up to something, and that something is to be constructed in the audience's imagination. Because it's in the imagination of the audience where the trailer is actually happening. Intrigue is not created with concealment—rather, it is created through reveal, a dropping of the curtain, a turning on of the lights.

The audience, after seeing the trailer, should already have a firm picture in their minds of what the evil in the film will ultimately be. That's why they show up. To have their biases confirmed— or disproven, shocked, and exceeded. When the trailer for THE

THING (1982) talks about "it" finding its way to our galaxy over a hundred thousand years ago, the audience starts kicking through its mind pre-historic beasts, creatures older than time. Dinosaurs come to mind. "But this is coming from outer space," the audience reasons. "And it can't possibly be coming here for anything good. But why now? Well, a group of unsuspecting scientists thawed it out…" The audience asks questions, leans forward, their minds hard at work. There's probably no greater imaginative leap in horror-film-marketing than in the trailer for SAW when the one chained man says, "He wants us to cut through our feet." The implication, horrifying. The rational, unfathomable. The question borne: "Will he actually go through with that?" Indeed, the trailer shows the man sawing away at… something. But what? The question is not 'Will he cut away at his feet?'—it's how. Audiences don't watch a SAW movie without knowing what will happen.

Like THE CONJURING, itself "based on a true story," as the trailer claims, suggesting events that have already played out, audiences showed not to see what would happen; rather, audiences showed to see how those true events would unfold. They wanted to see why the piano was playing by itself. They wanted to see why the one girl was tossed across the living room. They wanted to see how the young girls would react to the demonic ghost crouched above their dresser. Audiences wanted to learn what was in fact terrorizing that poor family. Audiences were already wondering how they'd behave in such situations. Better to see the film than be tortured by an unresolved imagination.

The audience wants information, not intrigue.

It is through revealed information that the viewer begins to build a mental model of the film, writing the movie in their own mind, needing to discover how it will all turn out. Robert Zemeckis (director of BACK TO THE FUTURE, CAST AWAY, and WHAT LIES BENEATH) puts it well: "The reason McDonald's is a tremendous success is that you don't have any surprises. You know exactly what it is going to taste like. Everybody knows the menu." People want to know what they're getting into—even if it is an experience of seeing a man hack off his own limb. The audience needs to know that going in, if only to brace themselves. They want to see the movie before they see it—the whole point in watching a trailer.

The trailer tells a scary story. It sells a scary story.

The point is inclusionary as it is exclusionary. The tossing of the girl across the living room (by her ponytail, incidentally) in THE CONJURING trailer, the man hacking away at his foot in the SAW trailer, the long explanation of the monster, is designed to keep people out as much as it is to bring people in. The filmmakers, the studio, whoever is behind the film, do not want people who don't like horror films showing up, and being disappointed—or worse, disgusted. Or even worse, outraged. The point of the preview, the point of revealing everything, is of the promoters putting their cards on the table and saying, "Beware, you're in for a scare." They want people to stay away as much as they want people to come in and take a peek—if they dare.

They want people forming concrete expectations.

Consider the trailer for INSIDIOUS. Right from the get-go, words on the screen say, "From the makers of PARANORMAL ACTIVITY and SAW." The audience immediately groans, knowing what's likely to come. "Hey, sweetie" a woman says to her child. More groans in the audience. "He's not in a coma," the mother announces of her son, "they don't know what to call it." A mysterious, sinister voice says, "I want it...NOW!" Want what, the audience asks? "I went into Dalton's room, there was something in there with him," a woman says. The implications play on the imagination of the audience. Now it's in kid's room? "I don't think bad wiring is the problem here" an expert surmises. "I wanna' leave; I wanna' leave this house" a woman gasps. "What is it?" someone asks. Through the selection and arrangement of exposition and actions, the trailer editor curated a presentation of expectations, visions of what the actual film would be—in this case, a horrifying examination of a family besieged by malevolent spirits. As written about in *How To Make Blockbuster Movie Trailers*, imagination creates expectation, expectation causes curiosity, curiosity causes the viewer to imagine, imagination creates demand. As McKee says, "skillful marketing creates genre expectation" (McKee, 1997, p. 90). ***Movie success is all about the creation of expectations. Phenomenal movie success is about exceeding those expectations.***

INSIDIOUS did just that, staying in the top ten for five straight weeks, declining only slightly, ultimately going on to spawn four sequels, the franchise itself grossing a half a billion dollars world-wide. The trailer created definite expectations, the film fulfilled those expectations—and then exceeded them in its execution of horror conventions.

INSIDIOUS is an example of a successful horror film. Not only was the trailer well positioned, but the film itself offered the goods—it spoke to the conventions of common horror films. It offered the materials for a great, expectant trailer; it then delivered on those promises with fresh insights.

But what does that mean? Well, for example, the trailer promises not just a horror film—but a ghost story. Specifically, the haunted house film. The trailer says this without implicitly stating so. Through a combination of dialogue, images, sounds, the film's trailer promises a movie about evil ghosts menacing a family, situating the film in a very specific niche of the genre. In the film, then, this is delivered on in fresh ways. As it being a ghost story, the audience expects a communication scene with the ghosts. Generally, the cliche is that a seance is held, an oracle makes contact. But in INSIDIOUS, it's done with the oracle wearing a gas mask, transmitting her whisperings via a pipe to someone wearing headphones.

This created an unusual effect, a different twist on a typical scene. Director James Wann and writer Lee Whannel, in other words, understood and understand genre. They are masters of the horror genre.

Not just in their demonstrated execution, but in their understandings of the horror genre's deep tenets. In the case of their film SAW, they knew enough that a horror film needed a killer—the twist is that the killer, in their film, never actually kills anyone. Unlike Freddy Krueger, unlike Michael Myers, unlike all the previous slasher-film villains, Jigsaw, the sinister evil behind James Wann's and Lee Whannel's film, uses his mind, not brawn, to kill. Wann and Whannel understood genre convention and came up with a fresh twist on the concept.

And while the trailer producer, editor, need not come up with the next Jigsaw, or a fresh twist on the horror genre (an excruciating, and increasingly difficult task), he must be able to recognize the phenomena of genre, of a movie's classification, of what makes it so, and what makes up its construction. He must not only understand genre inside and out, but he must also understand it beyond just superficial codes of using loud noises and jagged text. He must recognize the tenets as displayed by the film itself.

He needs to spot them, because he needs to present them—and them exclusively.

Creating trailers is a matter of selling a film. Creating trailers for horror films is a matter of selling the tenets of the genre.

Like James Wann and Lee Whannel, and as McKee says in his excellent book *Story*, the trailer producer must master the chosen genre. He must understand convention and cliche and know which ones to present—and which ones to ditch.

Therefore, it's imperative that a deconstruction of the horror genre occur. The following is that.

3

THE HORROR GENRE

Genre, as a whole, is a set of conventions. It classifies an entire set of stories. All films fall into a genre of one kind or another. Arguments about semantics aside, all films are genre films. In the case of horror, the trailer producer operates in a realm codified and structured by strict conventions and cliches, an accumulation of at least a hundred years of horror telling—and now, selling. The audience must be told, explicitly, that they're getting a horror movie, and what kind of horror movie they are getting themselves into.

Conventions

A convention is a precept that must occur for the thing itself to be part of a category. It must happen. No ifs, ands, or buts. Without it, the film becomes… something else. For example, in every horror film, there must be a source of evil. It can be, as McKee writes, of the uncanny, the supernatural, or the super-uncanny (McKee, 1997, p. 80). The uncanny is when the source of the horror is outrageous but subject to rational explanation—the alien, the monster made in a lab, the serial killer (McKee, 1997, p. 80). The supernatural is, as the name suggests, of the irrational variety, from the spirit realm (McKee, 1977, p. 80). The super-uncanny is a ping-pong between the two, where the audience can't be sure if the horror is actually rational or irrational.

A trailer will always elucidate whether it falls in one of the three cateogires, the categories themselves having categories and codes.

The Uncanny

First, the Uncanny. This is home to the science fiction film, the horror sci-fi, the slasher. This is the thing that arrived here "100,000 years ago" in the trailer for THE THING (1982). In this genre, especially in the trailer, the source of the horror must be identified and situated as soon as possible. The trailer for EVENT HORI-ZON, for example, situates itself in this aspect of the genre through several lines of dialogue. "This is incredible," the scientist says. The audience wonders what? "The Event Horizon." The horror is named—the film's setting, a spaceship. Already the audience suspects that this is THE SHINING in space. "The Event Horizon is the culmination of a secret government project to create a spacecraft capable of faster-than-light flight."

The Supernatural

This is the ghost film, the haunted house thriller. Movies like THE SIXTH SENSE, 1408. Again, here, the trailer must signal imme-diately that it's of this variety. "Standing next to my window," the Cole character in THE SIXTH SENSE trailer says of a ghost we can't see—yet. "I see dead people," the boy confirms. In the trailer for 1408, the narrator announces, "The afterlife became his obsession." A woman says, "So you're saying there's no such thing as ghosts." Yea, right, the audience chortles back. "Nothing would make me happier," the John Cusack character announces, "than to experience a paranormal event." His fate awaits in room 1408. "Ghostbusters," the narrator of the GHOSTBUSTERS (1984) trailer says, "they catch ghosts that won't stay dead." In all the trailers, the threat of the supernatural is named.

The Super-Uncanny

With this, the trailer must set the audience up to be unsure of what they're getting—at least, in the sense of it being something rational or supernatural. "Somewhere between science and superstition," the narrator of THE EXORCIST posits the audience. "He thinks the Klopeks are evil incarnate," the Tom Hanks character explains in the trailer for THE BURBS. "Well, you're much too smart to fall for that, honey" his wife warns. "Was it an accident? Was it murder? Was it a coincidence? Or was it…an omen" asks the trailer of THE OMEN. All of them hint at the horror vacillating between the supernatural and the uncanny.

Setting

Setting is a major convention that needs identified. Both in the film and the trailer. The horror film must take place somewhere, its place especially germane to the action that's to unfold. While completely devoid of dialogue, the trailer for ALIEN names its setting with the written words, "In space no one can hear you scream." A soon-to-be victim in the FRIDAY THE 13TH (1980) trailer asks, "What are you doing out in this mess?" He's referring to the woods surrounding him. "One of those big indoor shopping malls," a character in the DAWN OF THE DEAD (1978) trailer names. Audiences hear that and run through a mental checklist of where horror films have taken place—they discover "the mall" horror film has never been done. Their interest is piqued. "This is KBN Antonio Bay" a radio announcer says in the trailer for THE FOG (1980). "The Bates high school is alive with excitement," says the trailer for CARRIE. "Six strangers have been invited to a party" says the trailer for HOUSE ON HAUNTED HILL (1999). Where does it take place? In the house on Haunted Hill! The setting inspires the horror just as much as the monster.

Motivation

In all horror movies a motivation of the horror must be hinted at, especially in the trailer, especially in the uncanny and supernatural variety, as the force needs some reason for existing, and thus terrorizing its victims. "Someone who has seen one too many scary movies," claims the narrator of the SCREAM trailer—a clever twist in the 90s. "What do you want?" An exasperated girl screams at the telephone in the trailer for BLACK CHRISTMAS (1974). "He's waited for this night" Jamie Lee Curtis says of Michael Myers in the HALLOWEEN (2018) trailer. "He's waited for me." The scientist in the DAWN OF THE DEAD (1978) trailer explains of the zombies, "They kill for food. They eat their victims." In the trailer for THE PURGE, the motivations for making all crime legal for one night are laid clear: it "allows for a release." It's important to name motivation as early as possible because the audience is scratching its head as to why such a horrible force would exercise its presence. The motivation, in other words, adds authenticity.

Cut Off

Another convention is that the characters need to be cut off from society. The trailer needs to highlight this through visual cues or dialogue. Usually dialogue. "It's all down, all the lines," an operator in the SHUTTER ISLAND trailer says. "Do you know what we wouldn't have found, if we would have stayed on the trail?" A character asks in the trailer for WRONG TURN (2021), letting the audience know these characters have willingly strayed from society. "You see anybody?" The girl in the trailer for HOUSE OF WAX (2005) asks. Her boyfriend replies, "No, nobody." The trailer for YOU'RE NEXT relies on the visual of a car driving down a dusty road, entering the woods. "I just think I should be doing something about the rainforest," the girl in THE GREEN INFERNO trailer says, just before she ventures off to a place where no one dare go. All of this serves to prepare the audience to be cut off from civilization.

Of course, this is a convention of horror films where people go to places they shouldn't go. How about the opposite? What of a film like SCREAM? Or HALLOWEEN? Where the villains attack the characters in their own environments? How does the trailer producer signal to the audience that they too will be cut off? Of course, by including a scene where the character shouts for help—and fails to get it. The HALLOWEEN (1978) trailer shows the Jamie Lee Curtis character banging on the door of a house, hollering for someone to answer. The A NIGHTMARE ON ELM STREET (1984) trailer has Nancy shouting for help. The SCREAM trailer shows a shot of Sidney wrenching from the phone, failing to make a connection. I KNOW WHAT YOU DID LAST SUMMER (1997) switches out a young girl shouting for help, for characters trapped by a secret they can't tell anyone—this amply set up in the trailer. The same goes for SORORITY ROW

(2009)—the characters are cut off by a secret.

Collapse

Then of course, there are horror films where society itself collapses. This too has to be spelled out in the trailer, if only to signal that the film is taking place in another region of the horror genre—the *survival horror genre.* "Operator dead," a character in the DAWN OF THE DEAD (1978) trailer says, "Post abandoned." In the remake of the film, a news broadcaster says, "Officials have declared a state of emergency." This juxtaposed with images of burning cars and screaming, running people. "Seal the gates," a bad guy in the trailer for RESIDENT EVIL: APOCALYPSE says. "Execute code red," a military commander says in the trailer for 28 WEEKS LATER. All of these examples, among others, serve, in the case of survival horror, to collapse society, to tell the audience "There's no one left to call." It's no coincidence that all of the previous survival horror examples center around themes of communication. At any level of the genre, the trailer must reflect that the heroes of the film, the protagonists in question, are cut off from the society they are so used to. It serves to prepare the audience for the dark alley they're about to venture down.

All these conventions, distilling the type of monster, highlighting the setting, previewing the motivation, cutting the protagonists off from society in one way or another, all serve to construct a certain type of film. The horror film. Of course, there are basic themes that need presented—violence, for one. Chaos, for another. But these will trickle through in the course of presenting the other conventions. All of them serve to make up *the horror film*, all serve to ready the audience to see the same conventions they've become accustomed to over the years. It positions the audience, readies them, and conjures expectations about the fresh new ways those conventions will be filled.

4

THE PROBLEM OF RHYTHM

The trailer producer must establish the trailer's rhythm, the spacing between the dialogue arrangement. This is generally done by music. The trailer producer has a song he would like to use, he lays it down under the dialogue, and then he begins spacing out his clips of talk against the beat of the music, whatever that beat should be. This is an OK method for the trailer producer who owns, or who has access to, libraries of what are called "stock music," or even better, "real music," the kind used in other movies, other soundtracks, created by established composers. But that music costs money. Especially the songs by established composers.

Three Kinds of Music

First, there are three kinds of music: underscore, pre-existing songs, and music written for the trailer itself (ASCAP). Underscore is music without words—James Horner's score to ALIENS (1986) is one song trailer producers frequently use in horror trailers (namely the track, "Bishop's Countdown," with its anvil smash), Hans Zimmer's score to THE RING (2002), or Goblin's score to DAWN OF THE DEAD (1978). Pre-existing songs, and their master recordings, are generally songs with lyrics—Marilyn Manson's "I Put a Spell On You"—a track used in trailers like THE SIXTH SENSE and THE CABIN IN THE WOODS. Another example is "Hurdy Gurdy Man" by Donovan used in the trailer for THE CONJURING. Another is the excellent use of Rod Stewart's "(I Know) I'm Losing You" in the trailer for ZODIAC (2007), a song that perfectly captured the characters' hunt for the Zodiac killer. Music written for the trailer itself, for the film itself, is usually an original song by a popular artist or a remake of a hit song. "Ghost-busters" by Ray Parker Jr. is probably the most famous horror song written for a horror movie and, as well, incorporated into the trailer (although, it wasn't until late in production they produced the song. One of the prior teasers does not use it). Recently, the trailer for RESIDENT EVIL: WELCOME TO RACOON CITY highlighted an excellent remake of the song "What's Up?" by 4 Non Blondes, the song scrapping the guitar backing, and replacing it with orchestration.

It is especially temping to the trailer producer to reach for one of these kinds of songs. Nothing casts a sinister mood—and rhythm—of a trailer like the starting bass riff and drum beat for Marilyn Manson's "I Put a Spell on You." The music, without any words, just implies a force of unmitigated evil creeping across the landscape. As well, no song will make the trailer producer's job easier than Danny Elfman's main theme to BEETLEJUICE. No spooky song has been more overused (or underused?). It can be heard in every trailer that is parodying a scary movie—a la, SCARY MOVIE, as well as the trailers for CASPER (1995), and MONSTER HOUSE. It's a masterpiece of a song.

Pricing

But those songs cost. Especially for either a pre-existing underscore or song with lyrics. The ASCAP website lists between $15,000 and $60,000. However, these numbers are woefully conservative, especially for a hit song like "I Put a Spell on You"—and one, I might add, that may be tied up in a litigative nightmare due to it itself being a remake. The price is generally determined by the marketing budget of the film, or the film's budget itself, how the song is used in the trailer, the kind of film used—a studio piece, a student film—the license used, the duration of the license, the place of the license used (Brabec, 2007, ASCAP). All of these determine the final cost of the music.

For instance, if the film's marketing budget is especially high, the record company—whoever owns the song—will be sure to exact a huge fee. Think seven figures (Passman, 2017). Also, don't think that a small marketing budget will qualify for a discount. The request to use the song will simply be denied. It's not that record companies and famous artists don't like their songs to be used—it's that they don't want their song to be overused. Or, put another, they know the value of their hit song. They want to extract top dollar for their music. Can you blame them?

Duration

How the song is used in the trailer also determines its price. Does the trailer play the song the whole way throughout, therefore weaving its structure over top the song? That will exact a heavier fee than if the trailer only plays the song for a few seconds. Make no mistake though, that will be an expensive few seconds. Also, content comes into play. Does the artist "agree" with what's being shown in the trailer? Some artists, some record labels, may not want their song becoming the harbinger of doom. They don't want that very valuable master of "Strangers in The Night" becoming the anthem for a masked-maniac slashing away at scores of helpless co-eds. Or maybe they do. It all depends. Either way, someone will get rich over the transaction.

All Types

The kind of film, whether it's a studio film, a student film, a web series, a streaming film, plays into it. If it's a studio film, the record label will exact top dollar. If it's a student film's trailer, the record label will flatly deny the request. Put another way, if it's an independent trailer producer with no ties to Hollywood, the request, unless accompanied by a big check, will be refused, if acknowledged at all.

There is a "club" mentality to it; record labels only want to work with who they want to work with.

Duration of Usage

Another problem will be how long that trailer plans to be in use. Six months? A year? Two years? Forever? Of course, the trailer producer will want what's called 'perpetuity'—which is essentially eternity, or as long as the world lasts. Whichever should come first. The executives in charge of the trailer will also want this as well, as they do not plan to go through all this trouble of making a movie trailer, paying all sorts of money, only to have use of the trailer for six months because of a song buried somewhere in its run time. With movie trailers, it's perpetuity, or bust. Of course, perpetuity costs. In fact, that is what exacts such a huge fee. That and the final dimension of music licensing: territory.

Territory

Territory captures "where" the trailer, and therefore, the song, will be played. If it's only to be played in Benelux, the trailer producer can expect a steep discount on the song. If it's to be played in North America—and only North America—then the record company, whoever is doing the negotiations, will exact a higher fee. Of course, the fee is nothing compared to what it will be if the territory is "worldwide." And that's exactly what the money-people behind the trailer will want. Worldwide. They will expect, after going through all this trouble—again—that their trailer will be portable. They can pick it up and play it with peace of mind in North America, Europe, China, Africa, on and on. They will want to play it on the internet. They will want unfettered use.

The True Cost

To re-iterate an earlier point: music costs. It really does not matter the type of song—underscore, popular hit, elevator music, whatever—it will cost. And the cost will generally exceed the resources of the common trailer producer. Common because he is not "in the club" of Hollywood. Common because he's not "in the game," with the connections to establish use of a song like "Ghostbusters." There are many interested in parties in a song like that, and the trailer producer's trailer is more than likely not a part of those interests.

The trailer producer has to know this. Has to fully grasp that while music is wonderful, while it can take trailers to unspeakable, dazzling heights, music—copyrighted music, more specifically—exacts a steep toll on the budget of any trailer production. Hundreds of thousands of dollars, millions. Not to mention all the legal haggering that must ensue about territories and usage.

If anything can liberate and bog a trailer down simultaneously, it's music.

Stock Music

Stock music, on the other hand, offers an alternative, of course. And what's stock music? It's music "off the shelf," music created for the sole purpose of it being previously available for content creators to use at their leisure (more or less), at their need. The trade-off is that it's not as specific; it is more generic, more open to interpretation, more accessible in content. This bellies a flattening of the music. Whereas "Bishop's Countdown" was created for a very specific kind of scene in ALIENS, stock music, whatever song in question, was created to fill a convention in a genre. It was created, specifically, to be generic.

But stock music, as well, can cost. While its cost is a little more manageable, fees in the tens of thousands are not unheard of. Especially if the trailer producer requests of an artists to custom build a song. Companies like Brand X, Immediate Music, Audiomachine, Two Steps from Hell, and `, make some of the best stock music in the genre. While created to be generic, the company's listed music is certainly not generic. It is of a quality of the biggest hit song. These are professional artists churning out tracks specifically designed to elicit excitement, anticipation, and expectation. These are experts at the trailer music genre. Their music is built on the three-act structure, and solely on the three-act structure, with a quiet beginning, a ramped up middle, and an explosive finale. Their music is written specifically for the rhythm of a trailer.

Their music makes the trailer editor's job rather easy.

But with ease comes, again, cost. The trailer producer should expect, when working with one of those companies, or any popular trailer music artist, to pay anywhere from $5000 to $15,000, just as a conservative estimate. Popularity of the song's use probably comes into question.

Of course, there are artists just as good on other stock sites like Envato Elements. This is perhaps the best choice for the independent trailer producer, as Envato Elements offer music on a licensed basis. Meaning, the music is free to use, provided it is documented right.

The Real Point

The trailer producer should never lose sight that all of this is to establish a rhythm. He should never lose sight of this because, for one, it is easy to *lose sight of,* for another, because concerns of music, where it's coming from, how much it costs, whether it's legal or not, can trip up the designs of an otherwise competent trailer producer, editor. It's easy to get bogged down in music—or rather, rhythm. It's crucial to see the whole ordeal as rhythm, the music just a shading that occurs later. It's important for this reason: a trailer can still be cut without music. That is not to say the trailer will not ultimately have music, rather it's to say that the whole phenomena of music can be looked at from another perspective, from a fundamental, structural perspective.

Seeing Rhythm

In his book *Hearing and Writing Music*, Ron Gorow describes rhythm as a "relation of tones (notes) to the beat." (Gorow, 2000, p. 182). To grasp that, the word "beat" must be understood. That, in his book, is also defined as "the perceived pulse of the music." (Gorow, 2000, p. 182). Rhythm and beat couple to find more understanding in the concept of Meter, which is the "regularity of beats, divided into bars (measures)" (Gorrow, 2000, p. 182).

Rhythm, beat, and meter encapsulate the specter of music moving along in time. It also encapsulates the runtime of a trailer, its rhythm, which defines its beat, which is made up of a certain meter, which "is simply measurement" (Piston, 1987, p. 189). The words are another way of measuring the feel of a trailer's underlying structure.

Put another way, a trailer producer must understand the beats per minute of his trailer. He must recognize that trailers do not occur in time, but rather, in beats, and that those beats occur in measures, usually in cycles of four hits—1, 2, 3, 4—then repeat again—1, 2, 3, 4. The trailer's run time may factor in later, but for now, when establishing a rhythm, the trailer producer must understand the invisible tenets of music: beat, rhythm, meter. He must know how to ascertain a trailer's beats per minute.

To do that he reaches for a tool called a metronome. This is the device the Morgan Freeman character in SEVEN used to soothe himself to sleep. It's a chunky piece of wood with an upside-down pendulum that swings back and forth at a certain speed—the word "speed" a stand-in for beats per minute. For instance, 60 beats per minute, the device swings slowly—back and forth. 120 beats per minute, for instance, the device swings quickly, back and forth.

A metronome can also be found on the computer whether in the form of an application, or as a tool in a program like Logic Pro X or Abelton Live. As a standalone application, something that can be downloaded on a phone, it simply clicks out four beats—and then dings. "1, 2, 3, 4—1, 2, 3, 4." Each cycle representing a new measure—which is just another way of saying "bar," another term for a cycle, a measure of music. A metronome can also be found in Logic Pro X or Ableton; this is where the trailer producer will really need to find his beats per minute. In Logic Pro X, the metronome is located near the top, as it's the most important aspect of the program—or any musical program. It will generally be on a scale from 0 to 200; normally it will be found, by default, on 120 beats per minute, which is quite fast.

The trailer producer locates the metronome, then experiments. He notices that by turning "up" the metronome, it clicks faster. He notes that by turning it "down," it clicks slower. This is the essence of beats per minute, of capturing an understanding of rhythm, beat, and meter. It goes like this. The clicks represent beats, the beats make up the cycles of measures, the cycles and measures represent bars. For the trailer producer this means that an impact will occur with each new cycle, will demarcate each old and new cycle.

Time Signature

Each new cycle is determined by the trailer's time signature. The trailer producer needs to know how many beats are within each bar, within each measure. Again, "1, 2, 3, 4" represents a cycle, a measure. Then the cycle repeats. This is a time signature of 4/4. There are other time signatures. 5/4 is one especially germane for horror trailers. It stipulates those five beats will happen within each bar, creating an odd and uneven effect—perfect for horror trailers. This is, incidentally, the time signature of the theme song to HALLOWEEN. Some other time signatures that confer helter-skelter "time" would be 6/8 and 7/8. The trailer producer would be wise to experiment within these time signatures, as their usage will determine the feel of the trailer's rhythm.

Establish Speed

The trailer producer first establishes the speed he wants the trailer to move at. Again, slow is around 60 BPM (beats per minute).

Fast is around 120 BPM. Super-fast is 180 BPM. This is not to say that the entire trailer will be a single beats-per-minute. In fact, many beats-per-minutes will make up a trailer. The producer could start his piece at 60 BPM, letting it run for a few bars—then, he could shift up to 90 BPM, something more applicable for a rising tension. For the finale, he could ratchet the speed up to 120 BPM, the beat speaking to a frantic rhythm.

This selection of beats per minute can be "printed," rendered out as a sound file—and then that sound file is what the trailer producer edits to. Each beat represents an impact, each cycle represents a holding cell for a line of dialogue. This would be the same effect if an editor were using a piece of professional music, "editing to its beat." The only difference is that when looked at through a waveform, the professional music is all over the place, whereas the sound file of just the beats per minute shows a clear demarcation of where the beats are occurring, and where the cycle ends.

This makes "editing to the beat" a breeze. Which is why, even if the trailer producer has professional music, he should still ascertain the beats per minute of that professional music. He does so by putting it in a program like Logic Pro X, then finds the tool called the "BPM Counter," then plays a little bit of the tune; suddenly, a number will flash up. That is the song's beats per minute. The producer should mute the track and render out a two-minute clip of just the metronome clicking away. This gives the editor, again, a clear roadmap of where the song's beats are occurring, of where to place the impacts, of where to place the dialogue.

Through an understanding of rhythm, the trailer producer begins to grasp the fundamental precepts of music, and how it really operates within a trailer. It is crucial for the producer to understand concepts of rhythm, beat, meter, so that he can deduce the trailer's beats per minute. Doing so will provide a structural foundation to the trailer and point to exactly where that structure lies.

5

SCARY SOUNDS

The most important design of a horror trailer is its soundtrack. This includes music, to be sure, but so much of music and sound blend together that it's difficult to determine where one begins, where one ends. The previous chapter on rhythm is sufficient enough for music; this picks up where that leaves off.

The producer must invest a great deal in the production of a horrific—in a good way—sound design. He needs to listen—repeatedly—to the sound designs of other horror trailers, recognize how strategically designed they are. One example is apparent—in the trailer for remake of THE TEXAS CHAINSAW MASSACRE (2003), the sound designers augment the sound of a girl hollering for help as she runs around the house in the dark. The sound moves from one speaker, to the next. Then, when the villain "appears," his footsteps move from one speaker to the other. This is an extreme example, using a kind of self-awareness of the stereo fields to express an effect, but it's an effect none the less. In essence the trailer producer must use sound to communicate a series of ideas.

Horror sound design breaks down into seven categories. Rhythm, intensity, pitch, timbre, speed, shape, and organization (Sonnenschein, 2001, p. 65). Rhythm expresses the series of the sounds used throughout time. Intensity represents how hard, how soft a sound is "hitting." Pitch marks where the sound is falling on the frequency spectrum (a demonic voice would be a low pitch, for instance). Timbre is how the harmonics of a sound are working together. Speed is how quickly or slowly that sound arrives to the listener. Shape is the sound's envelope—a sound's envelope describing how that sound begins, sustains, decays, and fades away. Organization is the collection of all the sound effects in a trailer, their impart, their cohesion as judged against one another. From within those categories of how sound is defined, trailers utilize four different types of sound effects.

Rhythm

As discussed in the previous chapter, rhythm is what underlies the entire trailer itself. The selection and placement of the sounds makes up the content of that rhythm. Horror trailers rely heavily on the concept of rhythm. A great deal of the trailer for HEREDITARY is defined by the tongue clicks the Charlie character makes. Moments are shaped and defined by it. "I know my Mom would be very touched—and a little suspicious"—CLICK. This sound repeats throughout the trailer, creating a rhythm of unnerving tension, a tension that serves to act as a signature for the trailer itself. In the first trailer for IT (2017), the snap of the slide projector's carousel serves to act as an ever-increasing tempo to herald the clown's presence. The sequence climaxes with a very definite snap of the projector, then the sound serves to signal each and every title that pops up. This also informs a bit of the trailer's aesthetics—the title cards are interspersed with projector scratchings.

Intensity.

Sound "is measured in energy increments called decibels [dB]" (Sonnenschien, 2001, p. 66). A sound is either loud, quiet, or somewhere in between. Horror trailers use this concept to great effect. The classic example being the trailer having a cacophony of noise—and then stopping to dead silence, letting the audience edge forward on their seats in tension—only to have an unbearably loud sound scare the pants off everyone. The trailer for the M. Night Shyamalan movie SIGNS ends this way. The Mel Gibson character, outside of the cornfield, drops his flashlight. He reaches for it, only the sounds of cicadas remain. He has to hit the flashlight a few times to get it to turn on. A beat. More quiet cicadas—when suddenly, his flashlight catches the foot of an alien retracting into the cornfield. The soundtrack unleashes a host of screams, and a slam. The effect is to quiet the energy down so everyone listening leans in closer, their ears searching through the hiss for any kind of information. Their attention is "rewarded" by intensity. The ZODIAC trailer inverts this effect by quieting the mix, stopping the sound, signaling a boom, letting a creak get through the soundtrack, and having the Jake Gyllenhall character, standing in a dark basement, ask, "Are you sure there's no one else in the house?" There's a moment when the audience expects someone to jump out. But simply, the other man in the basement just turns off the light. Frustrating the intensity like this creates an unresolved tension that signals to the audience, "This is a movie about a monster who pops up, truly, at random."

Pitch

Sound occurs on a spectrum of frequency—20 Hz to 20,000 kHz. This spectrum also represents pitch. Sounds on the "low" end have a low pitch, sounds on the high end have a "high" pitch. The trailer for the remake of EVIL DEAD (2013) plays with this to great effect. When the trailer shows the possessed girl, it plays a "grinding down" effect, a tone moving from one pitch to a slightly lower one. As well, the "possessed" voices are achieved by lowering the actress' words, and then doubling them over, creating a hideous phasing sound. In the INSIDIOUS 2 trailer, after the one boy asks, "Is there something wrong with Daddy, Mom?" there is a power-down sound that lowers in pitch, signifying indeed that there is something wrong with Dad. Also, the trailer uses to great effect a "warbling" electronic sound that goes up in and down in pitch; it's used to underscore the singing of "Row, Row, Row Your Boat."

Timbre

Timbre is to what effect the frequencies of a sound are working together, creating either a pure tonal sound, or a noisy sound (Sonnenschein, 2001, p. 67). The trailer for THE PURGE is a great example of this, with its usage of a variety of warning sounds. Both the warning sound for the Purge itself, and the emergency broadcast system, together, create an unnerving timbre (and rhythm) that speaks to the ugliness, and messiness, of the events that unfold in the film. Conversely, the PREDATORS trailer utilizes a series of pure electronic tones that speak to the efficiency and technological sophistication of the monsters in the story.

Speed

While a complicated dense topic in of itself, it is basically how slow or fast sound travels through materials. Through air, sound moves fast. Through concrete, sound moves slow. A good example of this is in the teaser trailer for INSIDIOUS 3 when the young girl is tapping on her wall, thinking she is receiving "taps" back from a boy on the other side. The taps at first are marked by distance, the covering of the wall. The taps therefore are muffled, its "waves" smothered by the material within the wall. This effect draws the audience in, listening for more taps at that distance and speed. The segment climaxes when a hand suddenly appears above frame, accompanied with a very fast sound, one that's near and distinct.

Shape

The most important dimension of a sound is its "shape." The word shape assumes that a sound can be looked at from a two-dimensional perspective, seeing the beginning of that sound, the middle, and its ending. Its shape a model of the sound. The shape breaks into three categories—attack, duration, and decay. Attack marks how long it takes for the sound to really reach full amplitude. A scream would have virtually little attack as it just starts. An example is at the end of the trailer for DEAD SILENCE, as the man falls, as he tries to keep the scream in. The sound blurts right out of his mouth. Contrast that with another scream that begins with a slow attack, a slow "beginning," in the official trailer for HALLOWEEN II (2009), when the Laurie Strode character is asking for the nurse. That scream begins quietly, then picks up in intensity, volume, until it reaches full crescendo. Duration is how long the sound lasts. Again, a scream lasts a long time. A roar, as well. A hiss. A screech. Then, how long or short that song "fades" is its decay. This is the time it takes for that sound to lose its full energy.

Organization

Sounds can either be organized into two categories: coherent and incoherent. Coherent is when the sounds that play together come off as pleasing, relaxing. The beginning of a horror trailer typically organizes its sound around pleasant sounds, setting up a foundation to shatter with sounds that are disorganized, jagged, raw. The trailer for the excellent YOU'RE NEXT begins with a pleasant recording of Lou Reed's "Perfect Day." Then once the trailer takes a dark turn, the song is brought back and contrasted with slams, screams, roars, and all sorts of jagged, ugly explosions.

Once the trailer producer understands the dimensions of sounds, he moves on to recognizing that every sound in a trailer must do something—or, that the sound will achieve something. There are a variety of sounds out there—booms, whacks, hits, screams, screamers, zips, pings, dings—all sorts of names. But they all end up doing something, signifying something to the listener beyond just their content and placement. Their rhythm, intensity, pitch, timbre, speed, shape, and organization all unite to communicate signals to the viewer (the listener). Sound has to denote meaning that aligns with the communicative underlyings of the trailer's subtext, a subtext encircling everything from story to genre (Getty, 2022). It's in the sound's subtext where actual meaning will be found, not in its surface dimensions.

Therefore, all the varieties of sound effects heard in a trailer must be broken down into four categories. They are stops, impacts, accents, and risers. Stops do just that—they stop the trailer. Impacts do just that—they impact a certain moment. Accents, of course, accent whatever they play over. And risers—they link everything together, speeding everything up to an impact or a stop. Every sound falls into one of these categories, no matter how wild or chaotic.

Stops

A trailer needs a moment to breathe. It needs to "stop." A sound
that signifies this is simply called a "stop." It does what the name
suggests. It ceases all energy, forcing the viewer to take a breath,
pushing their brain to comprehend the message that was just delivered, and ready he or she for the new direction that's to come. In
the trailer for RED DRAGON, the Edward Norton character
says, "This one is gonna' go on and on." Suddenly a boom halts
all activity. The trailer is saying two things here. One, it is indeed
agreeing with Edward Norton's statement about the case going on
and on. But it's also saying that something deeper must occur. That
of the introduction—or re-introduction—of the Hannibal Lecter
character. The stop paves way, clears the path, re-routes all thinking capacity for the arrival of Hannibal Lecter. Another example
is in the THE CURSE OF LA LLORONA when the boy goes to
close the window, but it suddenly blows open (supposedly by the
ghost) and knocks him on the floor. The stop is twofold—the wind
hitting the window, the boy hitting the floor. The stop makes way
for the introduction of the trailer's copy. Stops serve as a traffic
cop, blowing a whistle, holding everything to a screeching halt,
allowing the way for more pertinent, deeper in quality, information
to be presented.

Impacts

A trailer needs to hammer home a variety of points. It needs to
"impact" moments. Hence the word "impact." This is where the vast
majority of trailer sounds will be found. It's in the impacts where
most of the evolution of horror trailers (and most trailers, for that
matter) can be found. Before the 1980s, trailers lacked distinctive
impact sounds, simply relying on certain shots (and their sound

effects) to convey impact. Now, especially after the 1990s, trailers impact almost every line of dialogue. Someone says something—boom. Someone hears something—bang. In essence, every line must be impacted. With the trailer for the Ethan Hawke horror film DAYBREAKERS, almost every line of dialogue is padded, highlighted with an impact. The Ethan Hawke character asks, "What happens when there isn't a single drop left?" there's a whoosh. "We only have a enough blood," a character informs, "to sustain our population to the end of the month." There is a flash sound. "We're talking about the extinction of the human race," says the Ethan Hawke character—there's a smash sound.

Accents

Moments in a trailer require accenting, hence "accents." These are sounds that provide not-quite an impact, not quite a punch, but rather, an underlining, an annotating. They clear the way for a bigger impact later. Nevertheless, they need marking; therefore, they need accenting. The difference between an accent and a full-fledged impact is subtle, very subtle. It's a matter of degree, and relativity. The purpose is to not wear out the impact sounds. In essence, it's a much more softened impact. In the trailer for SINISTER, when the one professor explains the nature of Bughuul's images, there is a warble sound that signifies a rip in the film. The word "images" is impacted because of its importance to the film's story. But it's not so impacted that the surrounding impacts aren't blunted, the surrounding impacts designed to shock and scare. In the trailer for LIGHTS OUT (2018), during one of the transitions, there is a "snap/click" to emphasize a shot of the house, which is of great importance to the story. The trailer, however, does not want to distract from the surrounding emphasis on the film's monster, so it saves the hard impact sounds for when presenting information about that. Accents simply, as the name suggest, accent. They provide a little bit of seasoning, a little bit of note—but not so much to interfere with later impacts.

Risers

Within each trailer sit sections, each climaxed by an impact or a stop. Usually a stop. The risers act as a means of speeding up those sections just as they near their finale. The "speeding up" sometimes comes from the nature of the riser to move from one low pitch to an upper pitch in one continuous movement, sliding through the notes, harmonics, frequencies, of that octave or octaves. Sometimes musicians emulate the sound via their instruments, their strings generally. Other times the riser effect is generated by a raising of the volume, an amplifying of the frequencies (making them fight with one another), addition of similar sounds, and a speeding up of the sound's frequency. Riser sounds provide the greatest amount of tension in the entire trailer; they are invaluable tools for deepening suspense. The trailer for ANNABELLE uses two types of risers, layered on top of one another. First, the general, which features a chorus rising in pitch, the chorus moving through the octave as the trailer flashes images of Annabelle's wrath. Layered on top of that is the sound of a music box, which increases in frequency as the riser nears its end. Risers serve to rev up the action just before the climax of the section in question, or, rather, and more commonly, with the trailer as a whole. They are one of the most valuable tools to a trailer editor.

Conclusion

The trailer producer must invest a great deal in the design of his trailer's sound. Nothing is more paramount to the success of the trailer, and the movie, than the sound design of the trailer. Although it can't be proven, one should examine what they believe to be the best movie trailer sound designs, and then compare that title with the film's box office numbers. One will probably find—and again, it can't be proven, because so much depends on subjective judgement—that the best, most thoughtful designs equal box office success. Take the trailer for THE PURGE, a trailer with excellent sound work, with a blurring between sound and music, with unique work not heard in any other trailer. Is that the reason the film opened at #1 with 34 million dollars? Maybe, maybe not. It sure helped. In my opinion, the films of the production company Platinum Dunes, the company that released THE PURGE, open well not just due to their quality, or the name recognition of the company's owner, Michael Bay, but because of the intense and unique sound work done on the trailers. The reader should go examine all the trailers of Platinum Dunes, note their sound work. Perhaps they are all made by the same trailer company, perhaps their sound designed by the same person. But they represent some of the best sound work in the industry.

That digression notwithstanding, the trailer producer has to go out of his way to use the tools available to create the best sound design possible. If horror is an effect on the psyche, then it's through the senses of hearing that those effects are amplified. Through an understanding of rhythm, intensity, pitch, timbre, speed, shape, and organization, the trailer producer can best organize his sound work. Also, through knowing the tools of stops, impacts, accents, and risers, the trailer producer can create an excellent soundtrack that will play on the fears of audiences everywhere.

The trailer producer should take note of other trailer sound designs—including the ones under the Platinum Dunes banner—and use the classifications of stops, impacts, accents, and risers listed in this chapter to figure out which ones in the trailers are which. The producer will note that not all trailers have all four—in fact, the trailer producer will note that trailers before the 2000s tended to not have risers. Indeed, he will note that the movies prior to the 90s, used shots, if they used them at all, to impact certain key lines of dialogue—not sounds. That is a relatively new practice. The trailer producer will learn a great deal about sound design by studying other good and bad examples.

6

EDITING

Editing is a subject that was covered extensively in *How To Make Blockbuster Movie Trailers*. But to reiterate here, editing is the assembling of disparate images into a whole. Really, it is the assembling of not just images, but of sound, image, and titles, the titles coming later. Editing is a subject examined from many different perspectives, but no sure-fire method has been discovered, or probably will be discovered. Editors can only offer what works for them and move on. Additionally, what makes editing so difficult is the nature of the job, and the result, itself. Editing, for it to work, must be made invisible. The audience must not perceive the editor is making a cut. The audience must, or at least, should, remain unaware that they're even watching a movie, absorbed into the experience before them. That is why everyone refers to it, like special effects, as the invisible art. It's so invisible, no one notices it. Shame. Because there are some really excellent editors out there who do yeomen's work, crafting motion pictures from countless hours of film dailies down to a watchable, and enjoyable, two hours. The task is unbearably difficult. Made no easier by countless interested parties yanking it this way and that way.

However, in trailer editing, all that changes. The edits must simultaneously be visible, and yet, retain enough of the invisibility of film-motion-picture editing. It's a contradiction. To put another way, the trailer editor edits to tell story—but also to shock, to direct, to sell. Editing a trailer is like super editing. It must be artful enough that it grabs attention, yet artful enough that the story gets through, that the message penetrates. The editor exists as star and stagehand congruently. As in trailer editing, the editor takes center stage—while orchestrating the stage. Confusing, making the job very difficult.

Editing a trailer is a unique affair. It requires a set of mental tools that go beyond just knowing how to use a computer. The following material assumes a great deal of knowledge about how to use a computer, and its respective editing programs; it's assumed the trailer editor already has a steady grasp of an editing software like Final Cut Pro X, or Avid, or Adobe Premiere. The material herein explores the philosophy, and as a result, the practically, of editing. The material examines how to edit a horrific movie trailer.

Organization

First, the editor must organize his shots. He must decipher them into two categories: impacts and pictures. Audiences and editors alike refer to these two types as "trailer-worthy" shots. Impacts are shots that, as the name suggest, impact. Pictures are shots that display interest according to photographic principles. Pictures can become impacts, but impacts are best used as impacts. The following explains the difference.

Impacts

Impact shots emphasize, exclamate; they impact. The editor places them directly after a line of dialogue. A woman in the trailer for LAKE PLACID says "Oh my god"—an alligator EXPLODES out of the water. "I hear something," a man says in the trailer for THE MIST—a strange bug slams the window. "There are like… people… or something living in those hills" a scared boy says in the trailer for THE HILLS HAVE EYES (2006)—a strange shadows swipes past the camera. The editor uses impacts to add an exclamation mark to his sentences.

What makes up an impact? A collision of some sorts. A connecting. Two disparate objects, shapes, lines, colliding in a single moment. The alligator exploding out of the water, the bug hitting the window, the shadow intersecting the light. The more of a collision, the deeper of a collision; the more resultant that collision ensues, the better. The gunshot, the scream (sound colliding with the mouth), the lightning strike, the punch, the monster pouncing, the monster snapping awake.

The more impacts, of course, the better. Unfortunately, movies only consist of so many. An editor will, generally, be only ever able to find about 10-15 in a decent movie. This of course will be just enough material to emphasize each line of dialogue in a trailer. In an average movie, the editor will struggle to find five to 10. Nonetheless—the movie has been made and the editor must work with what is actually there, not what one wishes for. The movie must succeed as a movie.

Most times, impacts will have to be invented.

This is where editing tricks come into play. The flash, the stutter, the speed-up, etc. These effects serve to add in the necessary collisions; these effects serve to do the colliding. For example, a woman in the trailer for THE HAUNTING (1999) gasps, "Oh my god, what is happening?" The trailer emits a slam sound effect and then cuts to a sped-up shot of a staircase.

The flash of a color can serve as a collision. Continuing with the example of THE HAUNTING, the trailer flashes a white screen, then cuts to a shot of the Owen Wilson character falling through the floor. If the reader examines closely, he or she will see that the actor's mouth isn't moving and that the scream was most likely added to beef up the impact. "I am so scared," the girl in the famous close-up shot of THE BLAIR WITCH PROJECT cries— then there are negative flashes of the film's title. In the trailer for SILENT HILL, the camera pushes in on an eponymous sign, just before it flashes to black and white. The effect is to say, "This is a really bad place!" In the trailer for UNDERWORLD, the Kate Beckinsale character says, "I'm beginning to believe the Lycans are following him," the trailer flashes a negative color of the character she's referring to, then cuts to the villain pursuing him. "I feel they were warning us," a character in the trailer for THE VILLAGE says, just before the screen flashes a negative shot of a door with the strange marking on it. Another excellent example is the trailer for the remake of THE AMITYVILLE HORROR (2005). "There's something evil in my house," the woman says; the trailer suddenly flashes a negative version of an anguished face for one frame, then the normal version of the shot for two frames. The flash of color is one of the classic ways collisions can be created out of nothing.

The stutter-edit is another way for an editor to materialize collisions. This is when the editor removes frames from the shot to create a rapid, staccato movement that implies more action than is actually there. The best example is in the trailer for THE SIXTH SENSE when the Cole character asks, "How do you know for sure?" and it cuts to a shot of Bruce Willis walking across the street. The editor removed several frames from the shot, so as to speed up the action of Willis' head turn. As well, the next shot of

a van careening at him is interspersed with empty black frames
to speed up Bruce Willis jumping out of the way. An otherwise
slow shot (slow because it's filmed from so far away), made more
action-packed by removing frames, and replacing with them with
just black. "I felt something was wrong," the character in THE
GRUDGE (2004) says. The trailer cuts to a shot of Bill Pullman
unaware of the ghost behind him—because there's no movement,
the trailer omits a number of frames, creating a flickering, or a
stuttering effect. In the trailer for the 2002 film THEY, the one
woman looks in a closet; suddenly it zooms in on her face and
omits a number of frames to quickly reach the part of the clip
where she screams into the light. The stutter-edit can be used to
speed up action, the black of the empty frames acting as adequate
collisions in and of themselves.

Pictures

The trailer editor then organizes shots into one place called, for lack
of a better word, "Pictures." This is structured according to photographic principles: Movement, balance, rhythm, pattern, emphasis,
contrast and unity. These seven categories define what makes for
"trailer-worthy" pictures. Of course, all seven won't always be found
in a shot; rather, the editor uses them as standards to recognize
and pick shots. The pictures are used as surrounding fodder for
the impacts, links, as it were to the next impact. They juxtapose
against whatever is being said in the dialogue.

Movement

Chief among all factors that go into pleasing, "trailer-worthy" shots
is movement. It stands as the most important quality of any of the

trailer shots, rivaling, almost, collisions. Movement directs the eye. Movement grabs attention; attention holds the audience through-out the entire trailer. Therefore, movement is a paramount quality. Movement centers around character actions such as running, head turns. In the trailer for the anthology film V/H/S, a woman talks at the camera; her re-adjustment causes the viewer to look one way, at her—then suddenly, the passing of a small figure drags the viewers' attention at it, causing for a startle. The trailer for V/H/S is chalk full of movement. The concept can also include movement from the camera—a character could be standing perfectly still, but the camera moving in on them creates a wealth of motion that captures the eye. Additionally, the camera dollying around the character or characters creates a parallax, a movement of both background and foreground—some of the most intriguing movement in cinema.

Balance

Alex White, in his book *The Elements of Graphic Design*, describes this as a state equalized by tension and equilibrium (White, 2011, p. 81). Balance is either achieved symmetrically, or asymmetrically (Jirousek, 1995). Symmetrical balance is when two sides of an image have equal weight (Jirousek, 1995). And, indeed, images can have weight. Not in any traditional sense. Rather an image can carry weight based on a host of artistic principles—value, for one. Black can be heavier than white, although white can be heavier than black. It depends on the value's relativity, what surrounds it, what makes up its balance. A symmetrical balance is when both sides of the image equal one another. The trailer for THE SHIN-ING highlights a famous example of symmetrical balance. Two red doors loom at the end of a hallway as the copy for the film rolls up the screen. The trailer for RESIDENT EVIL: WELCOME

TO RACCOON CITY showcases a number of symmetrically balanced shots. The first an overhead one of the S.T.A.R.S unit strafing into the Spencer mansion, a red carpet dividing the two equally placed members. As well, when they enter the mansion, two archways frame both sides of the staircase, which cuts right down the middle. Horror movies—movies in general—demonstrate a variety of symmetrically balanced shots. Asymmetrically balanced, conversely, captures images with a balance anything other than symmetrical. In other words, anything that falls on the grid of the rule of thirds, which divides the screen up in nine, equally spaced grids. The subject, again judged by weight, is placed somewhere on one of these axes. Continuing with the RESIDENT EVIL example, the shot that succeeds the one just described, a member of the S.T.A.R.S team looks out a window, shocked by something that's illuminating her. The camera places her on the upper right axis of the rule of thirds, providing an asymmetrical balance both visible and invisible to the eye.

Rhythm

Curating a showcase of movement, rhythm acts as a method of identifying a visual diagram upon which the eye puzzles through the image. Rhythm defines the shapes our eye moves through. The trailer for THE COLLECTION shows an image of five figures, all dressed in black, all armed with guns, aiming in the same way. Shadows fall before them; a window backlights them. The shot creates a rhythm of moving up and down, divided by light. Conversely, the trailer for PARANORMAL ACTIVITY 4 highlights an image that's subject defies rhythm: a black chandelier swings against a mostly beige background. While the chandelier moves back and forth, it's the doorway's frame that readies and directs our eye to real point of the shot: another chandelier plummeting right in front of the camera.

Pattern

Pattern, as the name suggests, represents a string of repeating forms. They can imply an emotional or intellectual series of repetition. The trailer for THE VOID opens on an image of a man dividing two equal rows of covered slabs—ostensibly covering bodies. The slabs are arranged in an almost mirrored pattern. Two by two. The trailer for THIRTEEN GHOSTS (2001) highlights a number of patterns—chiefly the geometric designs of the haunted house's many glass rooms. One shot shows them off clearly: lines intersecting with lines, intersecting with squares, squares making up lines of squares, squares making up other squares. The effect mystifies the eye.

Emphasis

Whatever catches the viewers eye marks the image's emphasis point. So much can make this effect occur; size, color, texture, shape (The J. Paul Getty Museum) Differentiation is the key. If a white square stands against a black background, the white square will draw the most emphasis. If a black square stands against a white background, the black square will draw similar emphasis. If a squiggly line rests between a bunch of jagged lines, the squiggly line will draw the most attention. In the trailer for THE HAUNTING IN CONNETICUT, a boy, sleeping, lit by candlelight, draws emphasis amidst a room absent any light.

Contrast

Sharing commonalities with emphasis, contrast examines differing shapes or colors, and how they relate to one another. A perfect example of this is found in the trailer for BEYOND THE BLACK RAINBOW, where the human shape of a young girl contrasts starkly with the unforgiving lines of a cold, lifeless airshaft, a black pit waiting at the bottom. The trailer for the film makes much use out of its young female protagonist, arranging her against many straight lines, all contributing to her sense of isolation.

Unity

The goal of all photography is to create a sense of harmony, of unity. The Merriam Webster dictionary refers to unity as "The state of being in full agreement," as well as, "A way of combining the parts in a work of art or literature so that they seem to belong together." In many ways it's the capstone of all the principles. In the trailer for THE UNINVITED, a shot shows someone running down a hallway; the balance and symmetry, as well as the other aspects of the shot, contribute to a sense of unity, everything harnessed around the reflected feet running across the tile. The feet are dead center in the frame.

Juxtapositions

Not all of these principles will show up in the same shot; indeed some of the principles overlap with one another. What is important is that the editor has some sort of guidance beyond just the collision of objects. He is looking to create a collage of interesting pictures, interesting defined by the previous principles. He applies these principles as he searches through the film, selecting images that meet these criteria, criteria of movement, balance, rhythm, pattern, emphasis, contrast, and unity.

The goal of collecting all these shots, of classifying them, is to make the job of placing them into the edit easier. Once the editor completes his collection more or less, he moves onto the stage of placing the shots into the edit. He does so mostly by one guiding principle: juxtaposition. Which is the concept of placing two ideas near one another, in order to create a third, unintended effect—a juxtaposition. Sergei Eisenstein and Lev Kuleshov created the concept. In the case of film editing, it's two shots placed together to create a third effect. For example, a shot of a monster looking, juxtaposed against the shot of a woman looking. The third effect is to have the monster staring at the woman. As written about in *How To Make Blockbuster Movie Trailers*, "It is a dialectic leap that creates a new qualitative attribute (Eisenstein, 1949, p. 72)." Editing movie trailers is all about crafting unique juxtapositions.

First, the editor creates juxtapositions around his impacts. Some examples. "I love you, Jimmy" says the woman to her boyfriend in THE STRANGERS trailer—suddenly there is a bang outside of their window, yanking their attention away from the intimate moment. The threatening sound juxtaposes their comfort and peace. The boyfriend instructs his girlfriend to run once he opens the door—an axe blasts through. In the trailer for ALIENS VS PRED-ATOR, one of the crew members shouts, "Let's go!" Suddenly all the doors shut, trapping them in. The one scientist asks, "What did you say this room was called?" The trailer somewhat answers—if in a morbid way—by showing the shot of a hatching egg, a baby alien unspooling from it. In the trailer for RESIDENT EVIL: APOCALYPSE, the Alice character narrates, "…trouble is, they didn't stay dead." Then, a shot of a dead woman, her eyes snapping open. In the trailer for RINGS (2017), the one woman says defiantly, "You're not real!" The trailer's answer? A shot of the TV set turning on, unleashing the ghost inside. The trailers do not need to name these juxtapositions; it's simply by their placement next to a completely opposite line that a new, unintended effect is created.

The editor then applies similar treatment to the "pictures" category. He finds a line of dialogue saying one thing, he locates a picture saying either its opposite, its contrast, or its direct underlining. In essence, creating a mosaic of juxtapositions. First, the opposite. In the trailer for THE HAPPENING, the news broadcaster announces, "White House officials claim the CIA has a defense against chemical weapons." The trailer, over the words, shows a picture of the Mark Wahlberg character looking at his terrified wife, implying that there is no defense to whatever is indeed happening. Then, the trailer editor finds something that contrasts what's being said. Continuing with the same trailer, the Mark Wahlberg character says, "Science will come up with some reason to put in the books." The trailer shows bodies jumping from a tall building, the shot certainly not showing science doing any work at all, except standing by and letting this terrible event happen. Finally, the trailer editor directly underlines, or rather, overlines, the dialogue with shots of what's being described. "She says everyone's dead outside," the one woman says; the trailer shows a shot of a huge aerial of skyscrapers, indicating that everyone out there is in fact dead. All three degrees of edits—illustrations, really—create degrees of juxtapositions. The editor works within these three types, overlaying the dialogue with the pictures. Generally, the trailer demands the direct underlining types of shots go first, as they are more on the nose, specific, germane to what is being said. Then as the trailer picks up meaning, the trailer allows usage of contrast, of contradiction.

While the impacts directly contradict, the pictures illuminate, illustrate, as well as contrast and outright contradict what is being said. The editor must not get hung up on picking the exact, correct shot. Rather, he moves quickly through his collection of impacts and pictures, placing them almost by instinct and feeling. Because it is a matter of feeling that juxtapositions speak to, of creating visceral reactions. That's what is key. Creating visceral reactions. Someone saying one thing—the opposite is shown—a third meaning registers with the audience. Someone says another—the trailer illustrates exactly that—understanding is had. A character claims one thing, its contrast is flashed—the audience takes away an additional meaning. The editor must pile on the juxtapositions, creating additional meanings that aren't exactly there in the images. Because it's through creating these additional meanings that the trailer editor stirs the imagination of the audience, involving them, motivating them to construct a plot, a story on their own, urging them to fill in the details by themselves. Juxtaposition is the main way to motivate a viewer to become involved.

Finishing Edits

After layering in all the shots, the trailer will begin to take over. By that, it is the trailer that will begin dictating the finishing edits. Some juxtapositions will not look quite right, or feel quite right, some pictures, where they've "landed," won't feel as "congruent" to whatever they're playing over. With these communicated feelings, the trailer is saying what it most wants. It is speaking to the editor to move shots from here to there, juxtapositions to this place or that place. The trailer editor should listen just as much as he edits, especially at this point. Editing, here, is more a matter of listening than it is a matter of cutting up pictures.

To aid in this listening, two concepts need to be touched upon, as they are perhaps two of the best concepts in editing, especially at this refining stage.

Blinking Eyes

First, the "blinking eyes" concept by Walter Murch. This postulates that editing is best done before someone on screen blinks. The idea is that the blinking bellies the thinking of the character, and that, if it is a good movie, that thinking should be shared by the audience watching, who also will be blinking in concert with the film. Whether this is true or not, the blink of an eye certainly catches attention, and trying to cut mid-blink will certainly cause some sort of subconscious discomfort in the audience. This holds true in almost all professional editing. Never will the viewer see a cut made mid-blink.

The Eye Is Quicker

Second, a concept coined by teacher Richard Pepperman from his book *The Eye Is Quicker.* His theory stipulates that an editor should generally cut on the blur of an image. Or, put another way, on the moment of maximum movement, the one that creates the greatest blur. Doing so will almost always hide the edit, making it invisible. For general edits, the intermittent edits between impacts, this is virtually perfect. If cutting to the beat, the images will almost always be visible and invisible at the same time—visible in a good way, invisible in the way that they aren't distracting the viewer, disrupting the message being communicated.

The two concepts, together, will provide all the necessary tools to really engage in the final editing of the trailer.

Trial and Error

Of course, further trial and error will be needed. The editor will have to make edits longer or shorter. Will have to "slip" shots a few frames here, a few frames there. But, more or less, the edits should just fall into place, provided the previous instruction has been followed. This doesn't mean that the editing will be easier, or that there won't be any thought; it means that, again, the trailer itself will dictate what it wants. The message the trailer is communicating will dominate the edits, will inform them to a large extent.

Conclusion

In conclusion, the trailer editor's main job is to find, collect, and categorize shots based on impacts and pictures. The impacts collide. The pictures are based on the photographic principles of movement, balance, rhythm, pattern, emphasis, contrast, and unity. Once the editor completes his organization, he then allows the trailer to speak to him; he listens and listens closely. He aids this final editing through Walter Murch's theory about cutting before or after the blink, and Walter Pepperman's theory about cutting on the blur, on maximum movement. The trailer editor also allows for some trial and error, moving edits this way and that way, until everything falls into place. Following this information will lead to editing that is both visible and invisible, that is artful, yet commercial, that will captivate and motivate the audience.

7

SPOOKY WORDS

Copywriting, sales in print, is what makes up the content of movie taglines, those words that pop up throughout a trailer. They also encompass any speaking done by a narrator—especially in older trailers. In more modern contexts, the characters in the movie do the speaking of copywriting. Sometimes their respective lines of dialogue do enough of the selling job. Make no mistake, however, a selling job must take place. And it must take place through copywriting, the content of a trailer's sales job. Copywriting must take place through the trailer's ultimate point of view: the salesperson. With any trailer, no matter how old, or how new, the trailer must be told through the perspective of not just the salesperson—but the *interested* salesperson. The atypical "company man" or "company woman" who cheerleads their workplace from the sidelines. Their work is done through copywriting, through the tools of hyperbole, through spoken or printed text, or through a character's words, provided such sales copy is made available by one of the characters.

The trailer's salesperson—especially the horror trailer's

salesperson—must take the perspective that the trailer before him is not just the scariest film ever made, it is the scariest film ever made about whatever subject it is about. The salesperson for THE TEXASCHAINSAW MASSACRE (1974), in the form of narration, reaches for the social proof of a critical review. "This is the movie," the narrator says, "that Rex Reed called the most horrifying motion picture I have ever seen." In more modern times, the salesperson, transferred over to the duty of doing the job through text, must come up with more ephemeral, creative ways of implying quality beyond just mere hyperbole. "Inspired by a true story," the trailer for the remake of THE TEXAS CHAINSAW MASSACRE (2003) reads. This is no longer just a film; it is an artifact reflecting reality at some level. It's another way of saying, "This is one of the scariest movies ever made—because it actually happened!"

Make no mistake, the salesperson must be behind all text, all voice over, all aspects of the trailer. He does this work through copywriting—whether that copy results in text or voice over. No matter the context, no matter the current styles dictating the modern mood of trailers (whether voice-overs or text are in fashion), the salesperson must appear somewhere in the trailer. The trailer is, after all, performing a sales job.

The trailer copywriter, the salesperson, will inevitably do their work through four tenets: character, setting, value, antagonism. The horror copywriter may use all four, but generally he emphasizes one over the other. He could mention all four, but emphasize character. Or he could, like most horror trailers, center the words around the antagonism. It depends on the quality of the movie, the audience's awareness of the characters in the film, their awareness of its events, of its contents. Sometimes a sequel is best sold around a familiar antagonism. Sometimes value must be spoken to. It depends.

Character

The copywriter may use character, which localizes all copy around the main character, or group of characters central to the story. The copywriter's words highlight the good of the characters in question, and their victimization, and their inevitable fight against evil. "The kids of Elm street don't know it yet," the narrator of the A NIGHT-MARE ON ELM STREET (1984) trailer says, "But something is coming to get them." In the trailer for THE SILENCE OF THE LAMBS, the narrator defines the Clarice Starling character as "A rookie FBI agent." "The one hope," the narrator for THE EXORCIST trailer booms, "The only hope: The Exorcist." The copywriter promises a fight between the eponymous character and the evil characterized in the trailer. It's rarer that a horror trailer will highlight the good forces, as they tend to be bland when in face of the horror in question. In other words, it's not as commercial to highlight the good. The copywriter must examine what is of most unique interest in the story. Consider the trailer for THE CONJURING. Its copywriter was faced between two primary forces—The Warrens, the good; the ghost, the bad. Between the two, the Warrens are by far the more interesting force. "Based on the true story of the Warrens," the trailer introduces.

Setting

Elsewhere, the copywriter may use setting to sell the movie. Setting breaks down into location and time; one of those two will be the primary slants. "It's the kind of house they don't build anymore," says the narrator of THE AMITYVILLE HORROR (1979) trailer, situating the film in a bucolic home. "A relic of a time when the world wasn't in such a hurry." The audience knows the kinds of horrors already present in it. The trailer for POLTERGEIST (1982) opens on an array of houses, the narrator saying, "The house looks just like the one next to it." Indeed, the house in question is unlike all the other houses. Using setting extends beyond the haunted house genre. In the 28 DAYS LATER trailer, the copy reads out a list of days, marking the onset of the apocalypse. The trailer for the remake of DAWN OF THE DEAD (2004) plays on its title, reading out a set of times from "evening," to "night," to "dawn." Setting provides great ambience upon which to situate a horror trailer in. The original HALLOWEEN, surprisingly, doesn't highlight its villain so much as it spotlights the time upon which the events take place—a la, Halloween.

Value

Another dimension to copywriting that provides ammunition for the copywriter is the film's value. This is to say "what's at stake" in the film's story. This is to say what is of most importance in the film. The copywriter will highlight this as the monster is either too general, or that there are greater things at stake than the terrorizing of just a few people. For instance, the trailer for the film FROZEN (2010), highlights three title cards that read, "Fight to survive." The value, obviously, survival. The copywriter uses this because the antagonism is a passive element, the cold; the characters can only hope to endure it. "Survive the night," the trailer for THE PURGE reads. The antagonism in that film more generalized than the trailer can speak to, survival the only hope. Horror trailers generally highlight survival as a chief value. Occasionally, horror trailers will speak to mystery, knowledge of some horrible event. The trailer for QUARANTINE promises this with its title cards reading out, "This fall, witness the shocking truth you are not meant to see." The trailer for SAW II promises an even greater mystery than the first one with title cards that read out, "The trap is set. The clues are hidden. The clock is ticking." In the trailer for SCREAM 4, the copy reads out, "Someone is re-inventing the game. Someone is re-creating the terror." The question is 'who.' Knowledge, the truth, the value.

Antagonism

In horror trailers, copywriters generally gravitate toward the film's antagonism to anchor their work. In horror films, the antagonism is generally the most interesting—or should be the most interesting. This is centering the trailer around the film's main villain. The reader would expect the copywriter to immediately triangulate all of his efforts around the evil force. But without audience awareness of the monster, the copywriter must build up the evil force from nothing. "There is a creature alive today," the narrator for the JAWS trailer starts out, "who has survived millions of years of evolution." The narrator goes on to sharpen the details of the evil force, never mentioning what specifically it is, as that would take away, only granting it description in the vaguest sense, saying what it does, at one time referring to it as the devil. "None of man's fantasies of evil can compare with the reality of… Jaws." The narrator in the trailer for CHILD'S PLAY never refers to the killer-doll by name, only citing words like "terror," "truth," only summing it up by saying, "There's nothing innocent about child's play." It's not until the sequel, CHILD'S PLAY 2, that the killer-doll becomes the star, the narrator saying, "This fall… Chucky rules." Generally, it's not until the sequel or sequels that the salesperson highlights the bad guy by name, as by then, the evil needs very little introduction. "Freddy Krueger is back on Elm street," the A NIGHTMARE ON ELM STREET 2 trailer narrator says. "Watch out for him!" This contrasts with the first movie's trailer, where the copywriter only highlighted the victims' fight with a generalized force. Amazingly, it's not until the trailer for the third FRIDAY THE 13TH movie where the famous Jason Voorhees is mentioned by name, himself now the star of the franchise. Even more amazing, it's not until the trailer for the fourth HALLOWEEN film that Michael Myers is identified by the copywriter: "Now, Michael Myers has come home." In trailer production, copywriting, the copywriter will highlight antagonism, mostly, in a generalized sense, only referring to it by name if the audience already has sufficient understanding of it (via a sequel or the original). The copywriter only uses the antagonism in either a general sense—for when the horror begins—or in a very specific way—for the sequel. Either way, antagonism serves as a major selling point for horror trailers.

Through either character, setting, value, or antagonism, the copywriter sketches a sales pitch for a scary movie, using one of the dimensions, or a combination of all four, to make a case to a potential audience. The copy not only making the case, but clarifying, specifying, buttoning up any questions the audience might have; the copywriter a helpful sales associate to all this. Through copy the trailer producer presents a compelling argument for the audience to actually see the film.

For a complete understanding of the concept, the trailer producer must turn himself into a legitimate copywriter. He must recognize what the concept of a tagline actually is: sales in print. Therefore, he must do the study. He must gather up the works of Dan Kennedy, Gary Halbert, David Ogilvy, John Caples, Drew E. Whitman, Eugene M. Schwartz, Robert Collier, Ted Nicholas, among many others, and do the reading, the listening. Through this study he will recognize the true essence of taglines, of the salesperson behind the trailer. Because not only are taglines sales in print, really, the trailer itself is like an audio-visual sales letter packaged and sent to the audience. The production of trailers is the production of sales letters. Only the trailer producer uses the visual, the auditory, to make his claims. He uses voice over, text to present his case. A mastery of copywriting serves as the fundamental skill for the trailer producer. It is imperative that the trailer producer become an expert salesperson.

8

DESIGNING TITLES

Once the copywriter writes the copy, the title designer must design the titles. This, of course, is usually the trailer producer himself, or, more specifically, the trailer editor. So often now a days, the efforts of trailer making, of post-production in general, falls into the hands of the editor. A great deal of the following material assumes this; therefore, the following material is presented as fundamentally as possible. It will be of great help to the editor when it comes time to design the titles.

To begin, movie copy, movie taglines, must be designed. It's not enough to just write out the copy and present it on screen. The words themselves require a great deal of styling; that styling done parallel to the surrounding aesthetics of the film, its content, the trailer itself.

The artist will confront two dimensions. The text and its background. The two will be worked on separately, then together, refining the two back and forth until they match—at least, match in a way that is pleasing to the eye. Text breaks down into a number of categories—font, size, kerning, leading, baseline shifts, vertical and horizontal sizing, and alignment, then color, which breaks down into its own categories.

Font

When creating text, the artist first examines font. This is how the text itself looks. In most programs, the default font is usually Times New Roman or Arial, which are, in most cases, to be avoided because, as being defaults, users not trained in graphic artists, tend to just use them as a matter of course. The users are not aware that the font can be changed—so they don't. But the trailer artist must change them. Or, at least, must consider changing the default font, and exploring all the other fonts available, not content until he explores all the alternatives.

There is a galaxy of fonts. All, however, organize around four categories: serif, sans serif, monospaced, and display.

Newspaper designers use serif fonts. As well, book, magazine, and instruction designers. Serif fonts confer tradition and readability. This is Times New Roman, Garamond Pro.

Sans-serif exist without the defining serifs at the edges of the words—they are sans, meaning without the serif. This is Arial, Helvetica.

Typewriters use monospaced font, a la what is called Courier.

Display fonts are everything else. Fonts used mainly for display purposes.

For horror films, a variety of fonts can be used. Anything that connotes horror, really. But what does it mean to connote horror? How is that done? Further, how is it usually done? While a variety of fonts can be used, graphic designers come back to a few classics. Trajan Pro is the most ubiquitous, used for such logos as SAW and ANNABELLE. The old challenger was ITC Serif Gothic, the font used in the HALLOWEEN (1978) trailer, a font that has seen a resurgence in recent years to replicate the retro horror feel. Graphic designers of retro horror titles generally reach for the ITC family—Benguiat Pro ITC the font for *Stranger Things*.

Size

The graphic designer must then consider how big or small the font is. Its size. Of course, this is relative to whatever else is on screen; it's hard to pin down a definition of "size." Just know that fonts can loom large or can barely register on the screen. Both types can be scary. For example, the text for title card in THE THING (1982) takes up the whole screen.

Tracking

When the title is considered as a whole, tracking examines how much space is between the words. The trailer for ALIEN (1979) leaves a lot of space between each word, suggesting the emptiness of the story's setting. Conversely, THE CONJURING has very tight tracking.

Kerning

Contrasted to tracking, kerning highlights the space between the individual characters, in that some spaces can have more space than others. This becomes especially apparent in a word combination like "AV" or "OW," the individual characters breaking into the other's space, which is defined by a square—not the shape of the letter.

Leading

Leading defines the space between each line. Titles with the word "the" deal with this, as the word "the" usually goes above. THE THING (1982), THE RING (2002), THE AMITYVILLE HORROR (1979, 2005), all demonstrate different leadings between "the" and the title itself.

Baseline

All text rests on a baseline. How much it shifts from that baseline is called a "baseline shift." Individual text can rest above or below this baseline. These kinds of shifts are most common when one letter is bigger than the next and has to be re-adjusted to fit.

Proportion

Font exists on a horizontal and vertical axis—the two can be individually shifted to create effects. Stretching out the vertical, for instance, will create a sense of paranoia.

Alignment

Text can be aligned relative to the edges. Generally, it's centered, although it can be "left" justified or "right" justified.

Font selection, size, tracking, kerning, leading, baseline shifts, horizontal and vertical proportions, and alignment all effect the total text design. They all have to be weighed against one another, judged individually, then judged as a whole.

Before color is added, the artist must first consider whether all of the previous adjustments line up with the film itself. He must survey the images of the film. Doing so gives spirit to the text, elevating it beyond just a bunch of numbers in a computer program. This is done through proportion, shapes, lines, and textures.

What kind of proportions are in the film? How big is the monster compared with the protagonist? Conversely, how small is the monster compared to the protagonist—as in the case of Chucky. Does the monster loom large? Is it stealthy and parasitic? This will have a great effect on the text itself.

What kind of shapes are in the film? Circles? Triangles? Of course, these shapes will be found in every film. But what tends to dominate the trailer in question? With talking heads—a drama—the dominant shape would be circles against some sort of angular background.

What kind of lines are there in the film's images? Is this for a horror film like BEYOND THE BLACK RAINBOW where the characters inhabit a world of strict geometry, or is this more like NIGHT OF THE LIVING DEAD (1968) where zombies come crashing through barricades, lending jagged edges to the title design?

What textures make up the film? This can be both literal and metaphorical. Literal in that the textures are primarily rough, jagged, a la the woods in the FRIDAY THE 13TH films. Metaphorical in the textures found in the story's rhetoric—chaos, bloodshed—which would infer a fraying of the titles. Irony could factor in contrasting the chaos and bloodshed with proper, angular text, as in the trailer titles for AMERICAN PSYCHO.

These of course are very subjective qualifiers, heavily dependent on ideas like irony and contrast. What's important is to be able to survey these qualifiers, work with them on a conscious level, as well as a subconscious.

Color

Color is one of the most important aspects of title design. What color will the text be? This is done through the dimensions of brightness, hue, and saturation. It's best to not make a title all white, and it's best to not make a title all black, as those two extremes suggest the designer isn't aware that those binaries exist as gradations. Although, this is not a rule. Colors connote a range of qualities. Symbolism comes into play. Although, the artist doesn't want to just play to the intellect, a la "The titles are red to symbolize the rage of the character." A nice thought, but does it look right when executed? Maybe. Maybe not. The title for THE EXORCIST (1973) trailer is red, although it could have very well been white, or, as on the poster, purple. Red was most likely selected to capture the evil that inhabits the young girl.

The Background

The text of the title must be placed on a background of some sorts. The artist needs to be aware that titles exist in a 3-D space, even if the final showing will only be in 2-D. And, even if movement is not used, the artist must consider the axes of all the elements. Is the text right on top of the background, or is the background pressed further away, creating an illusion of depth? Of course, placement isn't the only thing that creates depth. A dark halo around a white background suggests a spotlight, a deepening of the middle, a bowl for the text to be placed against. The primary purpose of the background is to direct the eye toward the text, to support the text.

In summary, movie titles must be designed. And they must be designed through the precepts of text and background, font, size, kerning, leading, baseline shifts, vertical and horizontal sizing, and alignment, then color. Then, the background is regarded in respect to proportion, shapes, lines, and textures. All of these weighed against the images in the film. Doing so will render pleasing blockbuster-level titles.

9

MIXING

Mixing is an essential process. It was covered extensively in *How To Make Blockbuster Movie Trailers*. To keep this focused on horror, the topic will be just briefly covered here again. Mixing is, unfortunately, mixing. But mixing must be done. The audio levels must be checked, dialed in, so everything plays at an even, while loud, level.

First, the trailer producer organizes his audio files. He goes through the project, separating dialogue, sound effects, and music into different categories. He can either tag these, as one can do in Final Cut Pro X, or he can separate them by layers. Either will do fine. It's important to play the trailer through to ensure that indeed only the dialogue plays with the dialogue, only the sound effects play with the sound effects, only the music plays with the music. This is so that, when others take charge of the trailer, they can swap out the dialogue with foreign dubs, or change the music in case such an occasion should appear. The organizing of the audio files is good practice.

Volume

Next, the trailer producer lowers the volume of the entire project to about -12 dB or -6 dB. Somewhere in between. He does this because, after adding in elements under the creative spirit, the entire project probably is playing at "full blast," already pressing the meter into the red. Dialogue should register around -12 dB, sound effects then, should punch out at around -6 dB. This, of course, is not an industry-shared practice. It is only from the experience of this author that these numbers serve to provide a quality mix. The numbers are to be taken with a grain of salt. They are just guidelines.

If these numbers are not achieved, then the trailer producer goes back and starts dialing them in individually. Of course, capturing numbers on a dial won't get the job done. Some pieces of dialogue will register at -12 dB, and then, on the speaker, barely register. That is to say, the producer can barely hear the audio even though it's registering on the meter. This happens. It means that the particular piece of dialogue needs augmented somehow. Either turned up in volume, or, because of its unique parameters, molded and shaped by a few audio tools.

Audio Tools

Two tools usually get the job done. The EQ and the compressor. First, the equalizer. If a piece of dialogue registers on the meter at a loud volume, but the content is barely discernable, it is more than likely due to unnecessary frequencies in the content itself. What does this mean? When a microphone captures dialogue, it records sound on a frequency bandwidth from 20 Hz to 20 kHz. Low sounds, rumbles, slow noise, hang around near the "bottom" of the spectrum, around 20 Hz. High pitched, piercing sounds, fast noise, reign at the top. If a clip of dialogue sounds quiet but registers at a high volume, it's most likely due to too much garbage hanging around at the bottom of the spectrum. The mic picked up too much "low end." Simply, the trailer producer applies an EQ to this specific piece of dialogue and cuts away anything below 80 Hz. Why 80? Because the male voice, the speaking of the dialogue, has a fundamental frequency from 85 to 155 Hz—i.e., this is where the content of the dialogue begins. Everything below 85 is just garbage noise. Indeed, the trailer producer can save a great deal of time by simply applying a universal cut at 80 to the dialogue track (and only the dialogue track) later in the mix. The second tool the trailer producer applies is a compressor. This lowers certain peaks of dialogue while raising others. It evens out dialogue. The nature of a compressor is beyond the course of this book; however, the existence of the compressor bears mentioning. The trailer producer should experiment with it. Again, a compressor will be applied to the universal settings of the track later, if only to even out the talk.

Getting Extra "Jump"

Once the trailer producer achieves an evenness with the dialogue, he then goes to the effects track and punches up certain sounds so they "jump" out of the mix. This takes a little bit of patience, as some sound effects will take up tons of space on the meter, climb up into the red, blow right past -12, -6, and still hide in the actual mix. It takes a great deal of finagling sometimes to get sounds to pop up in the mix without letting them take up too much space. Indeed, the trailer producer returns to the EQ and the compressor. If a sound takes up too much in the mix, without giving much in return, the editor can almost always be sure that it's due to the sound's low end. Here, the trailer does not "cut" at 80. He marks it around 80, and then lowers just that frequency.

The trailer producer should view frequency not as some alien concept, but rather, as a myriad of volumes that can be turned up or turned down. If a sound "takes up" too much space in a mix, but doesn't offer much sound in return, it's usually because one of its frequencies, almost always the low end, is capturing too much bandwidth. Every trailer producer should absorb this concept of multiple volumes, rather than just one volume, when it comes to mixing. The concept offers a great deal more control of the mix. Additionally, the trailer producer can use a compressor to control darting peaks, pieces of the sound that blow out the sound but offer little in return. The compressor can smash down these peaks, provided the correct threshold is achieved, and still retain the punchiness, the loudness of that sound effect, or music.

Final Mixing

Once the producer achieves an even balance, the dialogue just hovering right there with the music and effects—and hovering because effects and music will be mixed around the dialogue later on—he shuttles the entire project out to either another mixing program, or to three strips of sound that can be controlled: a dialogue track, an effects track, and a music track. They must be on three independent tracks and be able to receive universal controls of some sort. The producer could apply changes independently to each clip, but the process would become too much. At this stage, better to make universal changes. This is called the "final mix."

In a final mix, the trailer producer applies universal changes to the three independent tracks. To the dialogue, he applies a compressor, taming some of the wilder peaks of dialogue. He also applies an EQ filter, cutting off any frequencies below 80 Hz. Nothing should live there by the time the final mix rolls around.

When it comes time to mixing, the trailer producer, instead of going through and turning down the volume on the sound effects and mix, he instead begins to carve out frequencies. Again, rather than applying wholesale volume changes, he applies EQs to the sound effects and music track, pulling out frequencies that mirror the dialogue, creating a trough for the dialogue to sit in and pop out. This means that instead of just turning down the music or effects when the dialogue triggers, the trailer producer instead surgically goes in and turns down frequencies that the dialogue takes up, in effect not losing precious power in the music and the effects. As a result, allowing the low end of the music and dialogue to continue coming through, even while the dialogue plays. Wholesale volume changes would also, and unnecessarily so, turn down the "low end" on the music and dialogue. This way, important information that would have otherwise been thrown away can continue rumbling through.

The point is to clear, to carve, way for the dialogue. By the time the final mix is completed, the dialogue should "pop" right through, should hover just above the entire mix. To achieve the final effect, the trailer producer, the mixer, should turn the monitoring volume down very, very low—so low that only the dialogue is audible and just a touch of the music and effects can be heard. Then he should make his final mix. Then he should dial in his final settings. Once he does, he then turns the monitor back up—suddenly rewarded with a glorious mix where the music and effects punch through, and while the dialogue reigns as champion.

Mastering

The trailer producer, mixer, then masters the three tracks together as one. This adds a final polish, a competitive polish, to the mix itself.

He does this either manually with a series of filters—EQ, compressor, maximizer—or he applies a program called iZotope. The trailer producer, an amateur mixer, is advised to just seek out the program iZotope by Ozone and apply that. The program comes with a setting that will listen to the mix and then apply recommended settings. These settings are generally sufficient for a quality master.

The trailer producer than shuttles back his singular track and applies it to his trailer.

In conclusion, mixing is one of the most crucial steps in creating a blockbuster horror trailer—a crystal clear mix one of its rewards. It can be had by first organizing the dialogue, effects, and music into three separate tracks, then by moving those tracks to a separate audio editing program like Logic X and applying universal settings to the three tracks. The producer uses EQ and compression to achieve balance, eliminating any unwanted frequency in the dialogue track, and lowering respective frequencies in the music and effects tracks so the dialogue comes through. Doing so will produce an excellent sound mix. The producer then masters the three tracks together, adding a polish and shine to the final soundtrack. All of this will render a pleasing, final sound to the horror trailer.

9

"THE LAST MAN ON EARTH"

The following is a real-time commentary on the making of a horror trailer. The film used is the Vincent Price movie THE LAST MAN ON EARTH. I'm purposely not including a synopsis of the film as I've looked at it "cold." I've never seen the film and am only familiar with its source material *I Am Legend*. Like all trailers I produce, I know very little about what's in the film until it unfolds on the monitor. That's part of the challenge. In the following section, I examine the most important part of the film—the dialogue. I extract the most relevant dialogue from the film, present it for you to review, then I organize it into a final scripted trailer. The effect is to give you insight into my process of making choices during the trailer-making process. You're welcome to follow along with the exercise, doing the same work once the raw data is presented. My notes, again, are offered in "real-time" to show my thinking and how I react to certain developments as the process unfolds. Please don't take my thoughts as personal assessments of the film; they are just professional reactions to the content at hand.

The first thing to do is turn off the images. They will only interfere with finding the dialogue. The waveform of the dialogue's audio file will be used to select where the dialogue is. This is a little difficult as the source file contains dialogue, as well as effects and music. Normally, a trailer producer only works from a dialogue-only source. But THE LAST MAN ON EARTH is only available as is. So, first order of business is to locate the first piece of dialogue.

It's a good one.

                          VINCENT
                Another day to live through.

I splice, select, and raise that one out of the timeline. It's difficult to discern at first glance whether this is action or exposition dialogue—is he complaining, is the movie stating something? I would argue both. Something tells me I should take it.

At this point, I mention again that I am not familiar with the film THE LAST MAN ON EARTH. I've never seen it; I only have the foggiest notion of what the plot is. I've seen the other iterations of the Matheson story (THE LAST MAN ON EARTH is based on the novel *I Am Legend* by Richard Matheson), THE OMEGA MAN and I AM LEGEND with Will Smith, so I'm a little prepared in that regard. Although, it doesn't make much difference. The dialogue will tell me the story. I may not know exactly which dialogue to pick, and I will pick more than I need, but I will eventually ascertain the story from the process. "Another day to live through" just feels like something I should save for later.

I put the "scrubbing" tool on so I can hear the movie's sound at fast forward. Normally I would just eyeball where the talking occurs—but here, I have to wait till I hear Vincent Price's voice.

```
            VINCENT
December 1965.
```

This is for sure exposition, and it's an excellent catch. I may not use it, but it certainly tells me a lot about when the story is taking place. It also lets me know there's going to be a great deal of voice-over in this movie—maybe. It just feels like that kind of movie, what with there being only one character (for the most part). I'm already picturing using that line, pumping in drums. Maybe not.

```
            VINCENT
Is that all it's been since I inherited
the world?
```

```
            VINCENT
Three years. Seems like a hundred
million.
```

Remember, don't worry about all the music cues, all the sound effects. I can't repeat enough—everything beyond the dialogue, at this point, is a distraction from the core, the story.

```
            VINCENT
Yea, I own the world. An empty, dead
silent world.
```

```
            VINCENT
Everyday there are more of them.
```

This is a great line. More of what? My guess, the monsters. The vampires! This will be perfect for the trailer.

He says a line about not being able to afford anger—this is good. But it's followed up with the word "vulnerable." I wonder if I should take the time to lift this from the film. The word "vulnerable" isn't exactly trailer-worthy.

> VINCENT
> I've got to find where they hide during
> the day.

This describes an objective he has. I don't think it will make it into the trailer, but I'm going to save it, nonetheless.

> VINCENT
> Uncover every one of them!

> VINCENT
> Over three years, and there's more than
> half the city I haven't searched.

I'm getting an inkling that this movie will be very heavy on exposition, and that we'll have a great deal to choose from.

The line, "Those mirrors have to be replaced by dark." Exposition. But it's almost too specific. At this point, we're looking for something more generic. Vincent Price has such a great voice—I hope they gave him some ominous, quality words to speak!

It's at this point I start to make judgement calls about the film's quality. I start wondering if it's a good movie or a bad movie. I start picking it a part as I anxiously wait for more "story" stuff.

> VINCENT
> Four square blocks to search.

It's not great trailer material. But I might need it.

                    VINCENT
        How many of them still exist?

Bingo! This is important dialogue. It instills a question in the
listener. Who is "them?" Why are we concerned with how many
still exist!? Questions, questions.

                    VINCENT
        How long will I have to keep up this
        search?

                    VINCENT
        I haven't much time left.

Good exposition, stating a fact about the world he lives in. Could
be useful.

At this point, my subconscious starts wondering about music.
I hear the music in the film, which isn't a good thing to hear at
this point. But it makes me wonder about music. Pulsing synths?
Drums? With the story, I'm sensing it's about a world where something has gone wrong. Of course, I already know the story—but
even if I didn't, I would, at this point, be sensing that some sort
of abomination has occurred. Abomination makes me think of
scientific, which makes me think of a synthesizer. Maybe.

                    VINCENT
        12 long hours before the sun will rise.

                    VINCENT
            Drive them back to darkness.

That could be useful later, as a form of goal stating.

                    ZOMBIE
            Come out of the house!

At first, I thought it was singing on the jazz soundtrack, but
then I realized it's the film's zombies! I worry for a moment. The
zombies talk. For modern audiences, this is unusual. I capture
the dialogue for fear that the zombies will talk more and deliver
important talking points later on.

                    WOMAN
            Lord, I can't see! I can't see!

I don't know who is speaking this—whether zombie or human—
but it doesn't matter. It sounds dramatic.

                    WOMAN
            Lord!

She's begging the lord for help. That's its action.

                    VINCENT
            Another day.

                    VINCENT
            Another day to start all over again.

Shades of GROUNDHOG DAY come to mind. HAPPY DEATH DAY. It might be good to check those trailers.

> VINCENT
> The sun's already set!

> VINCENT
> They'll be everywhere!

> ZOMBIE
> Get him!

I avoid the zombie screaming, "Borgin!" I'm not even sure if I'm spelling it right. What's a Borgin? Of course, I know it's the character's name. But the audience sitting in a dark theater won't know that, nor will they care.

> VINCENT
> It's highly theoretical.

> GUY
> Theoretical?

A woman asks, "Is Europe's disease carried on the wind?" I'm tempted to pick this one, but I don't. I should. But something about it doesn't feel trailer-worthy. It's speaking to backstory, which is good. But it's the way the line is written, is said.

> VINCENT
> I'm a scientist, not an alarmist.

We're venturing into scenes where there's going to be a lot of talking. We really have to be vigilante to only pick the most germane pieces of dialogue; otherwise, we'll be swimming in choices, unsure of what order they go in.

Something tells me we're going to have to "go to text." That is something I always say when the trailer can't support only dialogue. Which is most of the time. The text are the titles that will appear later on, the voice of the salesperson, to tie the piece together. So, I start thinking at this point about text. What's the story so far? What other movies have a lone man pitted against the world? We have I AM LEGEND. THE OMEGA MAN. We'll definitely want to check out those trailers. But what else?

It is at this point that I start wondering about other movies, and how they were sold.

What other movies are like this one? NIGHT OF THE LIVING DEAD (1968). DAWN OF THE DEAD—both the original and the remake. All the countless zombie movies that are out there. I think of the most recent ones. TRAIN TO BUSAN. It'll be important to check that one. It's important because it's the most recent work speaking to modern audiences—it's what worked. And it will work again. Although we won't be copying directly. Never. We want to situate ourselves in the conversation that's already occurring in the audience's mind. What are they thinking about? And to be sure, they'll be thinking about TRAIN TO BUSAN, or whatever survival horror movie is most current. They'll also be thinking about DAWN OF THE DEAD, THE WALKING DEAD. We need to be prepared.

> WOMAN
> Is it possible this germ could be airborne?

VINCENT
The best brains in the world have been
running through this thing with a fine-
tooth comb.

What thing? Could raise some interesting questions. Of course,
"thing" isn't a great word. But it might be useful, and it might be
retrofitted a la, "The Thing." Who knows at this point?

Vincent talks more about the germ, but it's too scientific—for
a trailer.

WOMAN
I just wish someone would find a vaccine!

This is a good line, especially in modern contexts. It's impres-
sive they were saying those kinds of words even back then! What
a timeless story. I personally really want to use that line, as that
would speak into the current conversations going on about vacci-
nations—and will likely be going on when the film "is released."
That is to say, in our little experiment, in the here and now.

VINCENT
Everything is going to be alright
sweetheart.

Sounds ominous. Re-assurances are always great material for a
horror film. They never work out!

Just as I'm nodding off, listening to the dialogue, I hear this...

SCIENTIST
There has to be an answer.

Great line-read by the actor. He sounds desperate, authoritative.

SCIENTIST
You heard that all communications are
ended outside the continental limits.

At first, I'm excited about this line—then I hear the tail end of the phrase, "continental limits." Maybe this was how they referred to the United States when the film was released, maybe—I have my doubts—but it won't "sell" here. What are continental limits? The reason I like the earlier part of the line so much is it speaks to the convention in survival horror, which I'm suspecting this is where this movie lives, where all the communications fall apart. Perhaps someone with an authoritative voice could be hired to say, "All the comm lines are down." Although that was used in the SHUTTER ISLAND trailer. Perhaps something like, "The comm lines are failing!" But then that would speak to a progression, and more lines like that would be needed. Perhaps that's where the trailer is going?

There's two lines of thought here. A progression, and a stasis. A progression in that this film is actually about the progression of the disease, the virus—or, a stasis, in that the film "is about" the virus already having happened. I know the two are obvious, but which will the trailer fall on? Progression or statis? Do we sell to the audience that this is a story about an unfolding of the apocalypse, or about the apocalypse already being "here?"

This may sound out of left field, but it's a question that's going to have to be answered at some point.

Where is the story, in other words? The film is a mix of present day and flashbacks. But how do you communicate that in a trailer? Do you even want to communicate that?

These are questions that will cross your mind as you edit.

```
          SCIENTIST
The streets are swarming with truck-
loads of bodies that they're throwing
into that god awful pit.
```

This is a pretty effective line, but it's heavy at the end. Heavy in that it loses its purpose, or finds it purpose in something that needs more immediate explaining. I like that, "The streets are swarming with bodies!" Perhaps the word "truckloads" can be pulled out.

```
          VINCENT
You have a better idea?
```

```
          VINCENT
An unknown germ is being blown around
the world. It's highly contagious and
it's reached plague proportions.
```

There's a lot in this line. And it's, for a trailer, of course, a bit overwritten. I don't like the phrase "blown around the world." It evokes images of pinwheels and dandelions—at least, I think it does. But the line could be salvaged, if it's needed. And it could be needed. It describes "the germ." It could be salvaged by just using "an unknown germ." Then, "it's highly contagious." Cut. "It's reached plague proportions."

This is why it's best to make the trailer before shooting the film. A line in the script like that would be highlighted for trailer use, and then beefed up. It would be noted as extraordinarily important. Maybe "germ" isn't the right word. At least, not now a days. Germ is what they called "a virus" back in the 50s. I'm not criticizing; I'm aware that we're dealing with a movie made in the 1960s.

                        SCIENTIST
        And you don't believe some of the dead
        have come back?

What's this? It sounds like a very important line, for whatever
reason. It's said in the form of a question, but it could be re-fitted
in the form of a statement. Maybe. It builds a picture of what's
happening.

                          MAN
            Why are they burning the bodies?

Very evocative.

                          MAN
            Why don't they bury them?

                        VINCENT
            You'd prefer us to believe in vampires?

This requires surrounding context, but it could be chopped up
to just say, "Vampires?"

                          MAN
            There are stories being told, Bob.

Cut "Bob" and you have an interesting line, well-read, that
raises questions.

                        VINCENT
            By people who are out of their minds

with fear!

This could be re-fitted as "People are out of their minds with fear!" Maybe. Could be a really tight edit, but it might be helpful later on.

                    MAN
        Stories about people who have died--and
        have come back.

This is a great line.

                    MAN
        Why can't they stand the sunlight?

I'm for, whatever reason, thinking about the trailer to THE DARK KNIGHT RISES with its slow build and explosive finale? I'm thinking of the line where Anne Hathaway says, "Bane? You should be afraid of him as I am."

                    MAN
        Why are they only seen at night?

                NEWSBROADCASTER
        ...National disaster.

He says more before it, but the words could be cut. I'm thinking something like a channel flipping—those words flitting through the speakers with radio-tuning sounds.

                    CHILD
        Mommy, I can't see!

                    WOMAN
        I'm going to call the doctor!

                   VINCENT
        There's nothing they can do.

                    CHILD
        Mommy, help me.

                    WOMAN
        Please, for god's sake!

    I keep thinking about that question of progression versus statis.
Is this film about the progression of the apocalypse? Or its stasis?
    There's a lot of great line readings about the apocalypse—as it's
happening. The woman actress saying the previous line did a great
job with her lines. I could feel her pain. And if I could feel it, just
looking at a blank screen, just listening, then the effect will be
doubled on the audience when it's used in the trailer.
    Maybe. It might just have to be lost to stasis—i.e., the film is
predominantly about the apocalypse already having happened. I
wonder if I AM LEGEND used any of the story's flashbacks in its
trailer? Let's see…
    Yes, they did. They even started the trailer out with them.

                   VINCENT
        Are they all gone?

                   VINCENT
        Is there any hope from the latest

reports?

                    SCIENTIST
We'll find an answer.

                    VINCENT
When, doctor!?

                    VINCENT
Is everybody going to die before someone
finds the answer?

                    SOLDIER
Get behind those lines!

                    PERSON
I can't see!

                    ZOMBIE
We're going to kill you!

                    VINCENT
    It's alive!

   Listening to the dialogue, I'm reminded of the plot of the story,
and reminded that its plot wasn't the selling point. The situation
was. That's what was most unique about the story. Not exactly
the progression of events. This may prove challenging. How do

you make the situation interesting? The situation being the main character, alone in the world, wandering about the streets? A tough sell. This is why the I AM LEGEND trailer went to making a daily checklist for the Will Smith character, showing what he did with his day. That's the appeal. Then, of course, the trailer said something to the effect of, "The last man on earth…isn't alone." That's brilliant copy. And a brilliant appeal. We won't use that, for the sake of originality. But that's as powerful an appeal as any for the Richard Matheson story. The Will Smith version promised hours of chaos, of a battle between his character and hordes of zombies. The movie ended up kind of being that.

Something tells me this version will go in a similar direction. Which makes me think of our appeal for this film.

The twist, in the other versions of I AM LEGEND, is that he meets a fellow survivor. Which is a bit underwhelming when it comes to sales.

At this stage of the trailer work, one can't help but start to think about appeals. What's appealing about this material? I don't mean in the traditional sense, of "What's so appealing?" But in the true sense of the word—what's the appeal? The hook? The sell? What about this is different from the current market?

                         VINCENT
              They're dead.

                         VINCENT
              Someone else is alive.

                         VINCENT
              If someone can hear me, answer me.

                    VINCENT
          For god's sake, answer me!

                    VINCENT
          There, now we've got you all cleaned up.

This line gives me some hope. Who is he cleaning up? A dog? A mannequin, a la the Will Smith version?

                    VINCENT
          You know they're out there, don't you?

I'm beginning to really appreciate the trailer for the Will Smith version of I AM LEGEND. Not that I didn't before. But as I'm travelling through this terrain, examining the material for THE LAST MAN ON EARTH, I'm really starting to appreciate the work done on the I AM LEGEND trailer.

                    VINCENT
          Everything is going to be alright.

                    VINCENT
          No one's going to hurt you.

Listening to Vincent Price's voice, it just flashed through my head. It's a potential idea, and that's all it is. But: "Vincent Price… is the last man on Earth." Maybe. That's too obvious. But it's an idea. It's sort of an appeal, if Vincent Price were a star today, which we're going to, for the purpose of this experiment, assume he is. We'll assume he's right on par with a Bruce Campbell. If this film were made today, with a respective budget, it would star Bruce

Campbell, and be sold as a kind of EVIL DEAD apocalypse movie, which would be a really cool appeal. Not to give anyone any ideas.

> VINCENT
> Everything is going to be alright.

It sure makes me think of that song by Bob Marley—which, incidentally, they used in I AM LEGEND.

> VINCENT
> We're going to have lots of happy times together.

> VINCENT
> You'll see, everything's going to be fine.

> VINCENT
> What's the use?

> VINCENT
> Wait, I'm not going to hurt you.

> VINCENT
> Do you want to come with me, or do you want to face them?

> WOMAN
> You seem very well organized here.

                    WOMAN
You are alone.

                    WOMAN
Don't touch me!

                    WOMAN
Individually they're weak.

                    VINCENT
When I find him, I will drive a stake
through him just like all the others.

                    VINCENT
Perhaps I was chosen.

                    VINCENT
I have immunity.

  You never know what's going to be of value later on, so you save
almost everything that jumps out.

                    WOMAN
It's incurable.

                    VINCENT
There might be a way.

                      WOMAN
There are quite a number of us.

                      WOMAN
We're going to re-organize society.

                      WOMAN
Start everything all over again!

                      WOMAN
You're a monster to them!

                      WOMAN
You're a legend in the city!

                      WOMAN
Moving by day instead of night.

                      WOMAN
Leaving, as evidence of your existence,
bloodless corpses.

This line is good, but "evidence of your existence" should be cut.

                      WOMAN
Many of the people you destroyed were
still alive!

VINCENT

I didn't know!

WOMAN

They're coming after you tonight.

VINCENT

To kill me.

WOMAN

The beginning of any society is never
charming or gentle.

VINCENT

And you pretended to be shocked at my
violence.

VINCENT

You and I can save the others!

VINCENT

We won't be alone; we'll never be alone
again!

VINCENT

Don't be afraid.

It seems like the most effective lines are of the Vincent Price character trying to re-assure.

                    WOMAN
They'll come to kill!

                    VINCENT
Get away from her!

                    WOMAN
Robert, run!

                    WOMAN
They're trying to kill you!

                    WOMAN
Run! Run!

                    MAN
Up there!

                    MAN
There he is!

                    WOMAN
You don't understand! Wait!

                    MAN
Get him! Get him!

This is turning more into THE FUGITIVE!

                    WOMAN
    Wait!

                    MAN
    Move! Move!

                    MAN
    This way! Cover all sides!

                    MAN
    There he is!

I start to step back from the story, trying to get an overhead view
of things. The more and more I look at it, the more I appreciate
that copy, "The last man on Earth isn't alone." That's probably
some of the best copy ever written.

                    VINCENT
    You're freaks!

                    VINCENT
    All of you! Freaks!

                    VINCENT
    I'm a man!

> VINCENT

The last man!

And that's the last line of dialogue. Almost. There's a few after that.

Now, we review the chosen dialogue in one go. Taking it all in. Read through it. A new picture will emerge. Arrange it yourself if you care to.

> VINCENT

December 1965.

> VINCENT

Is that all it's been since I inherited the world?

> VINCENT

Three years. Seems like a hundred million.

> VINCENT

Yea, I own the world. An empty, dead silent world.

> VINCENT

Everyday there are more of them.

> VINCENT

I've got to find where they hide during

the day.

                    VINCENT
Uncover every one of them!

                    VINCENT
Over three years, and there's more than
half the city I haven't searched.

                    VINCENT
Four square blocks to search.

                    VINCENT
How many of them still exist?

                    VINCENT
How long will I have to keep up this
search?

                    VINCENT
I haven't much time left.

                    VINCENT
12 long hours before the sun will rise.

                    VINCENT
Drive them back to darkness.

                    ZOMBIE
Come out of the house!

                    WOMAN
Lord, I can't see! I can't see!

                    WOMAN
Lord!

                    VINCENT
Another day.

                    VINCENT
Another day to start all over again.

                    VINCENT
The sun's already set!

                    VINCENT
They'll be everywhere!

                    ZOMBIE
Get him!

                    VINCENT
It's highly theoretical.

GUY

Theoretical?

VINCENT

I'm a scientist, not an alarmist.

WOMAN

Is it possible this germ could be
airborne?

VINCENT

The best brains in the world have been
running through this thing with a fine-
tooth comb.

WOMAN

I just wish someone would find a vaccine!

VINCENT

Everything is going to be alright
sweetheart.

SCIENTIST

There has to be an answer.

SCIENTIST

You heard that all communications are
ended outside the continental limits.

SCIENTIST
The streets are swarming with truckloads of bodies that they're throwing
into that god awful pit.

VINCENT
You have a better idea?

VINCENT
An unknown germ is being blown around
the world. It's highly contagious and
it's reached plague proportions.

SCIENTIST
And you don't believe some of the dead
have come back?

MAN
Why are they burning the bodies?

MAN
Why don't they bury them?

VINCENT
You'd prefer us to believe in vampires?

MAN
There are stories being told, Bob.

VINCENT

By people who are out of their minds
with fear!

MAN

Stories about people who have died--and
have come back.

MAN

Why can't they stand the sunlight?

MAN

Why are they only seen at night?

NEWSBROADCASTER

...National disaster.

CHILD

Mommy, I can't see!

WOMAN

I'm going to call the doctor!

VINCENT

There's nothing they can do.

CHILD

Mommy, help me.

                        WOMAN
Please, for god's sake!

                        VINCENT
Are they all gone?

                        VINCENT
Is there any hope from the latest
reports?

                        SCIENTIST
We'll find an answer.

                        VINCENT
When, doctor!?

                        VINCENT
Is everybody going to die before someone
finds the answer?

                        SOLDIER
Get behind those lines!

                        PERSON
I can't see!

                        ZOMBIE
We're going to kill you!

VINCENT

It's alive!

VINCENT

They're dead.

VINCENT

Someone else is alive.

VINCENT

If someone can hear me, answer me.

VINCENT

For god's sake, answer me!

VINCENT

There, now we've got you all cleaned up.

VINCENT

You know they're out there, don't you?

VINCENT

Everything is going to be alright.

VINCENT

No one's going to hurt you.

                    VINCENT
Everything is going to be alright.

                    VINCENT
We're going to have lots of happy times
together.

                    VINCENT
You'll see, everything's going to be
fine.

                    VINCENT
What's the use?

                    VINCENT
Wait, I'm not going to hurt you.

                    VINCENT
Do you want to come with me, or do you
want to face them?

                    WOMAN
You seem very well organized here.

                    WOMAN
You are alone.

WOMAN

Don't touch me!

WOMAN

Individually they're weak.

VINCENT

When I find him, I will drive a stake
through him just like all the others.

VINCENT

Perhaps I was chosen.

VINCENT

I have immunity.

WOMAN

It's incurable.

VINCENT

There might be a way.

WOMAN

There are quite a number of us.

WOMAN

We're going to re-organize society.

                          WOMAN
Start everything all over again!

                          WOMAN
You're a monster to them!

                          WOMAN
You're a legend in the city!

                          WOMAN
Moving by day instead of night.

                          WOMAN
Leaving, as evidence of your existence,
bloodless corpses.

                          WOMAN
Many of the people you destroyed were
still alive!

                          VINCENT
I didn't know!

                          WOMAN
They're coming after you tonight.

                          VINCENT
To kill me.

WOMAN

The beginning of any society is never charming or gentle.

VINCENT

And you pretended to be shocked at my violence.

VINCENT

You and I can save the others!

VINCENT

We won't be alone; we'll never be alone again!

VINCENT

Don't be afraid.

WOMAN

They'll come to kill!

VINCENT

Get away from her!

WOMAN

Robert, run!

                    WOMAN
      They're trying to kill you!

                    WOMAN
      Run! Run!

                     MAN
      Up there!

                     MAN
      There he is!

                    WOMAN
      You don't understand! Wait!

                     MAN
      Get him! Get him!

                    WOMAN
      Wait!

                     MAN
      Move! Move!

                     MAN
      This way! Cover all sides!

MAN

There he is!

VINCENT

You're freaks!

VINCENT

All of you! Freaks!

VINCENT

I'm a man!

VINCENT

The last man!

Now we find the correct order of all this dialogue. This is the most challenging part of designing a trailer. I will introduce some combinations and see how they work. This is still an experimental stage.

VINCENT

Everyday there are more of them.

This is the first line my eye goes to. I hope I can build on it.

But quickly, I realize it's the wrong first choice. I wonder if the trailer needs to build a little. Do we want to open right off the bat? Or build? These are questions the trailer producer must ask.

I want to use this...

> VINCENT
> An unknown germ is being blown around
> the world. It's highly contagious and
> it's reached plague proportions.

...But the line isn't written right. It's too passive. The word
"blown" doesn't sit right with the genre.

> MAN
> Why are they burning the bodies?

> SCIENTIST
> And you don't believe some of the dead
> have come back?

Cut the part where he says "And you don't believe some of..."

> SCIENTIST
> The dead have come back.

This makes it a zombie thing, right away.

> VINCENT
> You'd prefer us to believe in vampires?

Cut "You'd prefer us to believe in..."

> VINCENT
> Vampires?

This skirts it away from 'zombies.'

MAN
There are stories being told.

VINCENT
By people who are out of their minds!

[Eliminated the words "with fear!"]

MAN
Stories about people who have died--and
have come back.

This might just be a step too far. I wonder if it could be re-arranged. Looking now, it all needs re-arranged. Some new combinations need tried out.

MAN
Why are they only seen at night?

CHILD
Mommy, I can't see!

MAN
Why can't they stand the sunlight?

This dialogue should be arranged so it says, "They can't stand the sunlight." I'm not sure if vocally it would work. But we'll try it.

MAN
They can't stand the sunlight.

WOMAN
I'm going to call the doctor!

VINCENT
There's nothing they can do.

There's a lot of dialogue to arrange. Try this…

SCIENTIST
We'll find an answer.

VINCENT
When, doctor!?

Then, maybe a little earlier in the trailer, contrast these two pieces of dialogue.

SOLDIER
Get behind those lines!

NEWSBROADCASTER
…National disaster.

Maybe there needs to be a little more build up, with some additional assets brought in. As I survey the lines, what jumps out at me is the unique angle that the victims of the virus first go blind. To my knowledge, that's never been done before. I keep this in mind.

There needs to be a front-end to the trailer. So, back up.

Re-surveying the material, I realize that the "present day" material isn't as interesting as the build-up. So, I attempt a build-up.

```
             VINCENT
   I'm a scientist, not an alarmist....
```

Jumps out at me.

So, as I survey the dialogue, I realize, again, the movie is in two parts. Pre-apocalypse, post-apocalypse.

After a while, I settle out an order of the dialogue. Here it is.

```
          NEWSBROADCASTER
   This national disaster...
```

```
             WOMAN
   I can't see!
```

```
            SCIENTIST
   There are stories being told!
```

```
             SOLDIER
   Get behind those lines!
```

```
             VINCENT
   It's highly contagious!
```

```
             WOMAN
   It's incurable.
```

```
            SCIENTIST
   The streets are swarming... with bodies.
```

SCIENTIST
...People who have died and...

SCIENTIST
...Have come back.

VINCENT
--Animal like. (This line of dialogue
had to be switched around)

WOMAN
I wish somebody would find a vaccine!

DOCTOR
We'll find an answer.

VINCENT
When, doctor!?

VICENT
Is everyone in the world going to die!?

VINCENT
If someone can hear, answer me!

VINCENT
For god's sake, answer me!

ZOMBIE

We're going to kill you!

WOMAN

There are quite a number of us!

WOMAN

They're coming after you!

ZOMBIE

There he is!

WOMAN

We're going to re-organize society.

WOMAN

Start everything all over again.

VINCENT

I've got to find where they hide.

VINCENT

...Uncover every one of them.

VINCENT

Drive them back to darkness.

                    WOMAN
The beginning of any society is never
charming or gentle.

                    ZOMBIE
Up there!

                    VINCENT
You freaks!

                    ZOMBIE
Get him!

                    VINCENT
All of you: freaks!

                    WOMAN
But you said he was your friend!

                    VINCENT
When I find him, I'll drive a stake
through him--

                    VINCENT
--Just like all the others.

Here is the final script, with "music" and "effects" placed in:

"THE LAST MAN ON EARTH" TRAILER SCRIPT

BLACK.
MUSIC: An ominous drone.
Glitch flashes.

          NEWSBROADCASTER
  This national disaster...

      NEWSBROADCASTER (ADDED IN POST)
  ...A virus.

Microscoped shot of bacteria, mutating.
Sound FX: squishes.

      NEWSBROADCASTER (ADDED IN POST)
  --reports of blindness.

             WOMAN
   I can't see!

Little girl in bed reaches out, eyes
saucered--stutter-edit.
Sound FX: Female scream--but from very far away,
wrapped in reverb.

          SCIENTIST
  There are stories being told!

A zombie woman approaches a terrified Vincent Price.

                NEWSBROADCASTER (ADDED IN POST)
            Mounting death toll!

Hands hold a clipped newspaper that reads "Plague
Claims Hundreds." Screen fritzes.
Sound FX: Smash, scream.

                    SOLDIER
            Get behind those lines!

A soldier fires.

                    VINCENT
            It's highly contagious!

Vincent, gas-masked, carrying a dead body. Screen
FREEZE frames on him. Sound FX: "cha" sound.

                    WOMAN
            It's incurable.

A dead body lays on the ground. Screen FREEZE frames,
flashes white.

                    SCIENTIST
            The streets are swarming... with bodies.

Zombies clobber a parked car.
Riser sound BEGINS.

                    SCIENTIST
    ...People who have died and...

Zombie throws stick.

                    SCIENTIST
    ...Have come back.

A zombie slams a stick into the side of a house.

                    VINCENT
    --Animal like.

Zombies grab at someone. Sound FX: Lion roar.

                    WOMAN
    I wish somebody would find a vaccine!

Vincent slams the door on a zombie's hand. Screen
flashes white.

                    DOCTOR
    We'll find an answer.

                    VINCENT
    When, doctor!?

Vincent emerges from darkness.

                    VINCENT
    Is everyone in the world going to die!?

Sound FX: Slam.
Riser ENDS.
Music: Drone STOPS.
Black.

                                                    FADE IN:

Sped up stock footage of sun setting.
Sun rises in distance.
Car passes deserted tanker.
MUSIC: Single string C Minor fades in.
Sound FX: Radio dialing through static.
Riser BEGINS.

                    VINCENT
          If someone can hear, answer me!

Static answers back.
Empty streets.

                    VINCENT
          For god's sake, answer me!

Sound FX: Slam.
Sound FX: Scream.
Music: STOPS.
Riser ends.

                    ZOMBIE
          We're going to kill you!

Sound FX: Whoosh.
Vincent Price, sitting on the couch, laughing.
TITLE: VINCENT PRICE

Music: Tense drum beat.

                    WOMAN
        There are quite a number of us!

TITLE: IS NOT

                    WOMAN
        They're coming after you!

TITLE: ALONE

                    ZOMBIE
        There he is!

Spot lamp flashes across Vincent Price's face.

                    WOMAN
        We're going to re-organize society.

Zombie smashes board through window.

                    WOMAN
        Start everything all over again.

Sound FX: Slam
Music: Stops.
Sound FX: Lightning.
Music: Full orchestra, tense beat. Drums pounding.

                    VINCENT
        I've got to find where they hide.

Vincent crafting the stakes out of wood.

                    VINCENT
          ...Uncover every one of them.

Vincent uncovers a woman hiding; she looks TERRIFIED.

                    VINCENT
          Drive them back to darkness.

He drives a stake down.

                    WOMAN
          The beginning of any society is never
          charming or gentle.

TITLE: VINCENT PRICE

                    ZOMBIE
          Up there!

TITLE: IS THE LAST

                    VINCENT

               YOU FREAKS!
TITLE: HOPE

                    ZOMBIE
          Get him!

Vincent, running up a staircase, fires back at a

zombie soldier.
Sound FX: Slam.
Music: ENDS.
Silence.

                                        FADE UP:

                    WOMAN
        But you said he was your friend!

Vincent punches a zombie.

                    VINCENT
        When I find him...

Vincent fires his gun.

                    VINCENT
        I'll drive a stake through him--

Vincent pounds another stake. Sound FX: SCREAM!

                    VINCENT
        --Just like all the others.

Sound FX: Slam, gunshot, knife-slice, scream.
Black.
TITLE: VINCENT PRICE IS
THE LAST MAN ON EARTH

CONCLUSION

Trailers are never easy to make, and horror trailers are no exception. They require patience, fortitude, and a wealth of education—of which the reader now has some access to. Of course, knowing isn't enough. The craft requires a lot of practice. Doing. And, re-doing. If the reader has a horror film, and wants a trailer for it, he or she needs to keep trying with the trailer, until it's done right. The reader will know when it's done right, and when it's not done right. The quality will either match the studio blockbuster trailers, or it will not. Of course, the reader is encouraged to keep at it, re-doing their trailer, re-structuring, going back through this book, re-reading, perhaps even reading *How To Make Blockbuster Movie Trailers*, doing all those steps until the quality of their trailer shines through the material itself. Because by following the tenets written in this book, the blockbuster spirit will eventually shine through any material. No matter its quality. That much the author can promise. One advantage the reader of this book now has over the thousands of other independent horror movies—indie movies in general—and the hundreds of other studio releases, is access to abilities that will coax out excellence from even the most under-developed material. Follow the tenets outlined, continue the work, and eventually the quality of any movie will come through, exhibited for the world to see.

Of course, the trailer maker has other options. If he or she feels trailer-making is not for them, he or she is more than welcome to email me at *tgetty1@gmail.com*. I am always available for consult, for clarification, for help, for service. I enjoy making trailers and enjoy even more taking on the most independent of movies, coaxing it out through the blockbuster tenets, and making a trailer that competes with even the best of Hollywood. I truly believe the marketplace belongs to the producer who has the best trailer, not the best movie. On that playing field, everyone can compete. Ancillary promotion come into play, of course. Promotion of the trailer is another thing entirely. But a quality trailer is a quality start. Remember, it's all about the trailer!

Best of luck.

Tom Getty

Tom Getty
March 6, 2022
Johnstown, PA

INDEX

TOM GETTY

Tom Getty is a movie trailer producer, and an award-winning writer, director, and actor, known for AMERICA HAS FALLEN (2016) and EMULATION (2010). He attended the University of Pittsburgh and graduated *cum laude* with a degree in communications. He creates professional movie trailers for film companies around the world. He can be reached at tgetty1@gmail.com

www.ingramcontent.com/pod-product-compliance
Lightning Source LLC
LaVergne TN
LVHW021454080426
835509LV00018B/2282